CUPS UP

CUPS UP

How I Organized a Klavern, Plotted a Coup, Survived Prison, Graduated College, Fought Polluters, and Started a Business

GEORGE T. MALVANEY

University Press of Mississippi / Jackson

Willie Morris Books in Memoir and Biography

www.upress.state.ms.us

The University Press of Mississippi is a member
of the Association of American University Presses.

First printing 2018
∞

Photographs are courtesy of the author except where noted.

Library of Congress Cataloging-in-Publication Data available

ISBN 978-1-4968-1679-5 (hardcover)
ISBN 978-1-4968-1680-1 (epub single)
ISBN 978-1-4968-1681-8 (epub institutional)
ISBN 978-1-4968-1682-5 (pdf single)
ISBN 978-1-4968-1683-2 (pdf institutional)

British Library Cataloging-in-Publication Data available

Contents

Preface

"Cups up, cups up!"

The voice boomed from the corridor on the other side of the bars, accompanied by a harsh rattling sound. I opened my eyes, still half asleep. Gray morning light seeped through the bars and across the thin pallet on my bunk, where I lay sweating in the humid air. It was still as hot as it had been the night before.

"Cups up, cups up!"

There it was again, closer this time. Maybe the meaningless words were the remnants of a nightmare; for a moment I hoped this was so, but the moment passed and I knew I was awake. I wished I wasn't. The rattling continued, interspersed with the subdued mumble of unintelligible voices. There was no one in sight. I was in solitary confinement because I was in transit to another prison.

I could see a slice of the corridor outside of my cell and that was it. Everything around me was gray—gray walls, gray floor, gray ceiling, gray pallet, gray bars. The air was ripe with the smell of unwashed bodies. There was no air-conditioning or even ventilation, and this was summer in Tallahassee, Florida. I'd been there less than twenty-four hours and somehow knew it wasn't going to get any better. It was worse than the Orleans Parish jail where I'd spent the last two and a half months in federal court proceedings, finally pleading guilty to conspiracy to invade a foreign country with the intent to overthrow the government. After sentencing I'd been put on a prison bus and driven to this federal prison. Even though it was late when we'd arrived, I'd been strip-searched and had a body-cavity check for contraband. It had been a long, exhausting day.

"Cups up, cups up!"

What the hell did that mean, *Cups up*? A prison orderly came into view, pushing a stainless steel cart along the corridor. Like me, he wore tan prison clothes, and also like me, he was white. His face was completely without expression. He looked old—forties at least.

"Cups up!" he barked. He waited a moment and asked, "Do you want any fucking coffee or not?"

Oh. I grabbed the cup I'd been given the night before and held it through the bars. He splashed lukewarm coffee into it and rattled on down the corridor. I stared at the coffee—it, too, was gray, just like everything else. And that's when it hit me, the blurry memories of the past few months: arrest, federal court, parish prison. It seemed surreal, like chapters in a book I'd only skimmed. But this cell in the Federal Correctional Institute in Tallahassee, Florida—this was the real thing. The night before I'd been too tired and overwhelmed to take it all in, but now it was clear. I was no longer George Malvaney of Jackson, Mississippi. I was Federal Prisoner No. 16691-034.

I sat on my bunk and took a sip of the coffee, which tasted horrible, thinking about the chain of events that had landed me here. How could this be happening to me? Where had I gone wrong? And how was I going to make sure I would never come back? Those were the questions I asked myself that morning. This book is about how I answered them.

PART ONE

George was born roaming.

—My father, **Louis Malvaney**

CHAPTER ONE

Nature's Child

Mississippi is a green state, full of woods and swamps and streams; they, in turn, are full of deer and snakes and ducks and rabbits and I don't know how many kinds of fish. I can't remember a time when I didn't love the outdoors and feel closer to the wildlife than I did to any person. When I was in the woods and swamps, I was free.

My father said I was a great storyteller, and he should know, because he was one himself. Some of the stories he told about me I was never sure were true—he had a propensity for embellishment until the truth got a little lost—but some of them I remember.

As a young boy, I drove my parents crazy because I had a habit of disappearing. My first roaming adventures were to see our next-door neighbor, a friendly older lady named Mrs. Morse. I don't know why I liked her, but it probably had a lot to do with cookies, or maybe it was because when I woke up during the night and went over to her house, she'd let me come in and visit. Sometimes I climbed into her bed; instead of throwing me out, she just called my mother to let her know I was safe.

One night when my parents found my bed empty, even Mrs. Morse didn't know where I was. After they had looked everywhere they could think of, a search party was organized. It didn't take long for someone to find me in the driver's seat of an abandoned truck in a neighbor's yard, hunched down in the seat with my legs stuck through the spokes of the steering wheel so that no one could see me. Another time, we were at a beach cottage in Gulf Shores and I went missing around daylight one morning before my family woke up. My parents became frantic, fearing that I had been curious about the surf, and notified the local fire department. They sounded the sirens and a team began searching. When everyone was close to tears, a man came walking down the beach with me on his shoulders. He'd found me a few miles away, tangled in barbed wire. My father said I was surprised about all the fuss and asked, "Why would I swim in my pajamas?"

I also liked to visit the country store near our family farm where old men gathered to tell stories. I told them stories of my own, which they seemed to enjoy. According to my father, I called myself the Old Friend, perhaps as a way to ingratiate myself to them. Around that time I discovered that the Shell station near our home on North President Street was another good spot to sit around and swap tales. After a while, my mother would phone the station and tell whoever answered to send me home. I never liked being cooped up. I wanted to be out doing things. In this regard, I haven't changed much.

I discovered the woods and swamps early. When I was ten, the other neighborhood kids and I began building forts out of pine limbs in the woods near our homes. We taught ourselves the ways of the woods and the animals that lived there.

When I was twelve, I told my parents I wanted to camp at the Pearl River, a short distance away. My mother wasn't keen on the idea, but my dad backed me up, saying, "Hell, that boy can take care of himself better than I can." Other kids in the neighborhood—Tim Jacobs, Kirk and Todd Hines, Bill Cooper, Jack "Lick" Lind, and Pete and Bill Savage—camped with me. We hunted squirrels with pellet guns and cooked them over a fire; on a few occasions, we even caught and cooked cottonmouth water moccasins.

One Friday night Tim, Lick, and I got into a bit more mischief than we had any business doing at such a young age. The Coopers, who lived next door to Tim, were gone for the night. Bill Cooper was our age, and he had shown us the stash of *Playboys* that his father kept under the bathroom sink. We decided it would be a good idea to climb through Bill's bedroom window and sneak a look at them. Once we got to the bathroom, however, we changed our minds, figuring that we'd take them for our permanent viewing pleasure. We each scooped up a stack before going back out Bill's window. When the Coopers returned home, they discovered they'd had visitors, and it didn't take long for them to find out that the three of us had been spotted outside of their house at night. Mrs. Cooper called our parents and told them what she suspected, and then my father found the *Playboys* under my bed. I got one of the worst whippings I'd ever received and had to apologize.

Along with pictures of naked women, I was also fond of snakes, especially venomous ones. I was a risk taker, thrilled by the idea of handling live, venomous snakes. I learned that if you put a snake in the freezer for a short period of time, it got too sluggish to move quickly, which made handling it easier. Then when you took it out and lay it in the sun, it gradually regained its ability to move normally. But my mother didn't like reaching into her freezer and encountering a coiled water moccasin, so she made me stop. Instead, I'd just walk out of the swamp with a snake curled around my arm, knocking on neighbors' doors to scare the ladies who opened them.

My dad taught me about guns and how to hunt for small game, mostly squirrels. When I was about six, my father began taking me squirrel hunting with him. I absolutely loved to go hunting with him and couldn't wait until I was old enough to have my own gun.

Opening presents on Christmas morning in 1970, I found two neatly wrapped boxes, small but heavy. I ripped the paper off to find two boxes of Peters shotgun shells. When I turned to show my father what Santa had brought me, he handed me a long, padded case that I instantly recognized. I eagerly unzipped it and pulled out a 20-gauge, single-shot Stevens shotgun. I was thrilled beyond words.

The following day we went to a friend's farm, and I practiced by shooting cans placed on top of fence posts; that afternoon we squirrel hunted along a creek that flowed through a stand of hardwood trees.

My father had brought his double-barreled shotgun but allowed me to be the sole shooter. I killed two squirrels and was hooked for life. Before long, I was hunting rabbits, wood ducks, and other small game.

On New Year's Eve in 1972, however, my love of hunting nearly ended my life. My mother had driven my friend Bob and me to the end of our street and dropped us off for an afternoon of hunting in the Pearl River swamps. By now I had graduated to using a double-barreled 20-gauge shotgun. Bob was using a double-barrel that belonged to my father, but he was used to a pump gun where the safety is in a different location. We were hunting out of a twelve-foot johnboat, with me in the front and Bob about eight feet behind me. I'd just leaned over the front of the boat to paddle when I heard the loud boom of a gunshot and felt the shock of the blast. I vividly recall looking forward and seeing my hat fly through the air as if in slow motion and then gently land on the water.

My mind raced as I tried to figure out what had happened. Dazed, I stared at my hat floating on the surface of the water and then noticed a red stain forming around it, but I couldn't come to grips with what was happening. I knew something was wrong but could not comprehend what it was. I had felt a tremendous blow to the back of my head, and my ears were ringing. And then a searing pain hit. I reached up and touched the back of my head; my hand came away bloody.

"You shot me," I said to Bob. I began to regain my composure and knew I had to get to land. We started paddling toward shore, though not before retrieving my hat.

We were over a mile from the nearest home and had no choice but to walk out. With each step, the pain increased, and I could feel the warm blood running down my neck and back. We finally made it to the nearest home, the Draffens, and they called my parents and began applying towels to the back of my head in an attempt to slow the bleeding. My parents arrived a few minutes later and immediately placed me in the backseat of our family station wagon. My father was driving, while my mother sat next to me, holding me tightly as we sped to the nearest hospital, St. Dominic's. She kept reassuring me, in as calm a voice as she could muster, that I was going to be okay.

I was rushed to the emergency room, where a neurosurgeon removed seven pellets from my skull; three pellets had penetrated the skull and come to a stop adjacent to my brain, where they remain to this day. I was so close to the muzzle of the shotgun when it discharged that the plastic wadding inside the shell actually knocked a plug out of my scalp. The neurosurgeon told my parents that it was a miracle I was still alive. I had been shot in the head from a distance of only about five feet; if the barrel had been just a quarter of an inch lower, I would have been hit with a fatal load.

For the next few years, I wore that cap whenever I went hunting, even though it was missing its top and the rest of it was covered in blood. There is still a bald area on the back of my head where the scar tissue prevents hair from growing.

I achieved even more notoriety a few years later when I reached into a rotten stump, the roots visible under the ground. I'd told a friend of mine, K.C., that places like this were where snakes hibernated in the winter, and if we pulled up the stump we'd probably find one in a root hole. So we rocked it back and forth until it was loose, and I reached down to grab hold of a root. Instead, I pulled up a copperhead with one fang embedded in my right middle finger. K.C. told me to jump on his dirt bike so he could take me home, but it felt safer to me to walk after being bitten by a venomous snake.

By the time I got home, my finger and hand had swollen to twice their normal size. Back we went to the St. Dominic's Hospital ER, and I spent a couple of days receiving antivenom and immersing my finger in ice until I couldn't stand it. The neighborhood kids thought it was pretty cool that I was tougher than a copperhead. My parents just shook their heads.

I also learned about nature in more normal ways. Like my older brother, Sam, who attained the rank of Eagle Scout, I joined the Boy Scouts. The scoutmaster, whom we referred to as Colonel Cabaniss, didn't take bull from anyone. He was a tough, no-nonsense ex–US Marine; when Colonel Cabaniss talked, I listened. He taught us how to make a fire using only one match and what he called "squaw wood" (fine wood shavings). I enjoyed the camaraderie of Boy Scouts and particularly liked the camping trips, but unlike my brother, I earned no merit badges. Despite my admiration for Colonel Cabaniss, I just didn't care about rank or any kind of structured environment where you had to follow rules. It was more important to me to learn the ways of the woods and swamps and discover my own rules.

In my early teens, I developed a love of coon hunting. A family friend, Arnold Dyre, had two bluetick hounds, Maggie Mae and Billy Pup, and was an avid coon hunter. Mr. Dyre and I spent many a night in the Pearl River swamps, but we rarely if ever killed the coon once it was treed. What I loved was the thrill of the chase and listening to the dogs baying.

To me, *home* meant the outdoors, not the house I lived in or the people who lived there with me. I know this makes me different from most folks. I tended to keep my family at a distance, and when I look back, I can't say that their influence played a large part in my life. I didn't like feeling crowded or tied down by expectations. I felt closer to the animals and snakes than I did to my brothers and sisters and even my parents.

My family didn't feel at home with me either. They were an expressive bunch, in love with drama, and though my odd behavior provided them with many opportunities to indulge this love, they couldn't seem to figure me out. Their disapproval was always there. My mother continually tried to put the brakes on me and keep me within her tight boundaries. The older I got, the more suspicious she became, and I gave her many worried nights. Sam was into stuff that bored me silly, and vice versa. I viewed my two older sisters as nothing more than girls and tried to ignore them as much as I could. My younger brother, Christoph, saw me as a way to get attention by ratting me out to our parents whenever he got the chance.

I gave him lots of chances, and as a result we were usually at odds. None of them seemed to feel the same need for freedom that I did. For one thing, they all loved school and did well there, and they had little interest in outdoor pursuits like hunting, fishing, and camping. They were indoors people. It's no wonder we weren't close. The only people in my family who seemed to approve of me were my father's parents. I admired my grandfather, who died when I was ten. He had a presence about him, like he always knew what was right. He was a prominent man in the community, an architect who designed many landmark buildings in Jackson and around the rest of Mississippi. He's still remembered today with respect.

I also loved and admired my grandmother, Nana, a fireball who always spoke her mind. She was strict, too, but I liked that because I always knew where I stood with her. When I was young, before my grandfather died, I'd spend the night at their home on Terry Road in South Jackson. Nana would get up early in the morning to make biscuits with Sue Bee honey for me before sending me outdoors to play. She could control me better than anyone else because she demanded respect. I had to say "Yes, ma'am" and "No, ma'am," and if I forgot, she'd haul off and wallop me (or at least threaten to). I wasn't afraid of her, though. My grandparents meant a lot to me because they approved of my need for freedom, my love of nature, and my desire to be active. I know I was a tough kid to raise, but my grandparents thought I was just fine.

My grandfather owned a relatively large plot of land near Hopewell, Mississippi, about an hour from our home—more than seven hundred acres of swamps, oxbow lakes, bottomland hardwood timber, and upland fields on my beloved Pearl River. Some of my fondest childhood memories are set at Hopewell: hunting squirrels, ducks, quail, doves, and rabbits; fishing; frog-gigging; catching snakes; playing in the swamps; and learning the woods. I developed a deep appreciation for nature and the environment that eventually led me to become a passionate and dedicated environmental regulator.

Outside of my grandparents, the person I was closest to in my family was my father. He also liked to be busy "doing stuff," and he enjoyed the outdoors—not as much as I did, but we could communicate. Also, I think I fascinated him. I certainly gave him a lot of material for stories. My father showed me how to use nature and how to protect it so it was always there.

My father's favorite thing was fishing. He began taking me night fishing when I was about ten years old, and we'd go when the moon was full, making it easier to cast around tupelo gums and cypress trees in the lake. We used a top-water lure called a Jitterbug that had a wide mouth on it. When you reeled it toward you, the wide mouth caused the lure to make a steady *plop-plop* noise that attracted the bass as it moved across the surface of the water. It was exciting to be reeling the lure toward you—listening to the sound of the Jitterbug and the crescendo of nature's music made up of crickets, frogs, owls, and whippoorwills—and have a bass explode on your lure in the darkness in front of you.

My father liked peace and quiet and being able to talk about what mattered to him. He was a wily devil, so he used this time to preach to me about the value of education. As a professional engineer who worked at my grandfather's architectural firm, Malvaney & Associates, he wanted me to do better in school because with an education I could get a good job and my life would be easier. He was right, of course, and if I'd listened to him I could have avoided a lot of hard times, but I brushed off his words as if they were mosquitoes.

Because I hated being cooped up, school was a big problem for me. I hated it—really hated it. Sitting still in a desk, not being able to leave when I wanted, breathing stale air, listening to an adult babble on about unimportant things—my God, it was horrible. I passed the time staring out of the window and daydreaming, wishing I was outdoors where things were happening and lucky people were doing things. Like the Scout merit badges, I cared nothing at all about grades; to me, a D- was a good grade because it wasn't an F. I rarely studied or did any homework unless forced to do so by my father. Most days when I got home from school, I headed for the swamps.

When I was twelve or thirteen, I saw the movie *Jeremiah Johnson*, starring a young Robert Redford. I didn't like movies much because they were all sitting and watching, but that movie spoke to me. It was about a guy who tried to get away from civilization and live in the woods with only grizzly bears for company. Other people gave him a lot of trouble, but he defeated them all and was allowed to live his own life, the way he wanted. Nobody cooped up Jeremiah Johnson. He knew how to be free. I wanted to be just like him. Unfortunately for me, though, it was 1972, not 1850.

CHAPTER TWO

Cultural Lessons

ississippi went through a lot of changes during the years I was growing up. When I was in elementary school, I paid little attention to what was going on in my community, and what was happening in the rest of the country might as well have been on another planet. If it wasn't taking place in my woods or swamps, it didn't matter to me.

The central issue was race. I lived in a polarized society divided along racial lines, which I took for granted when I was young: that was simply the way it was.

But then things started to change.

In the early 1970s, just as I was entering adolescence, there was a lot of discomfort for southerners, both white and black. Change is always uncomfortable. Many white people felt angry and frightened by the social changes forced on them, but at the time I wasn't aware of how strong those feelings were. I simply absorbed the attitude of the people around me. I would not describe it as animosity, however—not in my family or with our friends. It was merely the perception that black people and their culture were different from ours and should be separate.

Even today, Mississippians still have a tendency to self-segregate—churches, schools (public versus private), and social functions are often organized along racial lines. There are exceptions, of course, but this is the reality. Despite this, most black and white Mississippians get along with one another just fine—much better than the national media and people outside of the state give us credit for.

I was raised in an upper-middle-class neighborhood in a family that has a long history in Mississippi, especially in Jackson. My grandfather literally helped build the city where I grew up. I am a sixth-generation Mississippian and very proud of it. My parents were known and respected in the community. We had ancestors who fought in the Civil War—on the Confederate side, of course. I have no idea whether or not our ancestors were slave owners. Maybe there were some, but I don't know about them; I never asked, nor was I told. It wasn't important.

One of my father's oldest friends and classmates at Central High School was Sam Bowers, who became notorious for his affiliation with the 1960s-era Ku Klux Klan, although the two men were not particularly close as adults. Another family acquaintance, L. E. Matthews, was also associated with the 1960s Klan. This wasn't discussed, however, at least not in front of the children, and I didn't learn about it until years later.

I don't remember any racial animosity coming from my parents, my grandparents, or any other members of my family. My contact with black people was minimal. There were no black families in our neighborhood, and I didn't hang out with any black kids. We had a black maid, Leola; she and her mother, Liza, worked for us for years, and I was fond of them, but I can't remember ever talking to them about race or politics or anything personal. The adults in my life must have had opinions about the events of the 1960s and 1970s— the marches, the racial violence—but I don't remember them ever talking about it.

School integration wasn't discussed, either. Integration began when I was nine or ten, and when you're that young, you just accept things the way they are.

The social upheaval of the times made no impression on me until I entered Bailey Junior High in seventh grade. My elementary school, Casey, had been integrated when I was in fifth grade, but it was a slow process, and there were only two black kids in my class. This hadn't bothered me, probably because I didn't give it much thought, but at Bailey the changes became personal.

Bailey had been integrated two years before I arrived—an all-white school had suddenly changed into one that was 80 percent black. Most of the black kids came from the poor inner-city neighborhoods of Jackson, and in several of my classes I was one of the few white kids. Because of my upbringing, I had no experience at all with black kids my age or institutions that catered to them. I was thrust into a culture that was totally alien to me, and with no preparation, I had no idea how to handle it.

There were some rough and violent black kids at Bailey, many of them from single-parent homes that had values very different from mine. They cursed a lot, started fights, and ganged up on anyone who made them angry, even the teachers. Many seemed to have no respect for anyone. I had never been in that kind of environment before, and I didn't like it. I wasn't raised that way; I'd been taught to respect my elders. You definitely didn't cuss around them—the idea of using crass language in front of my mother or grandmother was unthinkable. And as far as fighting or hitting an adult, that was like science fiction or something.

My father had also gone to Bailey. He'd even had the same coach I had. Coach Stowers didn't like the new Bailey either, particularly the lack of respect for authority. He carried a fiberglass rod—a CB antenna with electrical tape wrapped tightly around one end—that he used as a whip. If anyone, black or white, got ugly with him, he'd pop the kid with it—whack, right across the bottom. He tried to demand respect but had little success with some of the meaner kids. They weren't afraid of him or his rod. One time, a bunch of them threatened to jump him and beat him up; they were stopped by the other teachers, but it showed how little they cared. I liked Coach Stowers, who was only trying to enforce discipline.

Bailey had little discipline or structure. My elementary school might have been boring, but at least it had been organized. Bailey was like being inside of a real Animal House. There were rules, but they weren't enforced. Although some students managed to focus and work hard enough to receive decent educations despite these things, I wasn't one of them.

In response, I began to make judgments. It wasn't that all the black kids were bad—the majority of them were okay people—but it seemed to me that all the bad people were black. Looking back, it's clear that most of them were just as upset about the changes as I was, but at the time I didn't think like that. I wasn't exactly anti-black, but I started developing a racist attitude. I suppose I was afraid, though at the time I was aware only of a simmering anger.

My indifference to racial issues evaporated at Bailey. I began to take sides. But at first it wasn't really about race. It was about a culture I couldn't identify with and anger about being forced into an environment in which I didn't belong. I saw another movie around this time, *Billy Jack*, that summed up my resentment. Billy Jack was a half-Indian guy fighting the ranchers who owned all of the land (who, by the way, were white). I think the movie resonated with me because Billy Jack fought for innocent people who were being forced into a culture that was bad for them—just like me, right? Naturally, I didn't see that the black kids had been feeling the same way—when you're thirteen, there are no shades of gray. I felt like I had to pick a side or get trampled on.

I didn't blame all the black kids. I'd talk to them in the hallways or in class, and we'd be friendly with one another, but we didn't get together after school; we didn't invite each other over to our houses. I was friendly with one black kid, Jeffrey, who liked airplanes and knew a lot about them because his father was a pilot. I liked airplanes too, though I'd never been on one. I liked to read about the air battles of World War II, and Jeffrey and I had some long discussions about those warplanes. We didn't talk about anything else, though, and certainly not the racial tensions at school.

Bailey did not get better over time, and my grades, which were never good, got worse—almost all Ds. The only reason I didn't get Fs was because they didn't flunk anyone. If they had, many of the kids would have failed. So I passed my classes, but the only thing I learned was how much I hated school and especially how much I hated Bailey. I was only there for a year and a half when my parents pulled me out and sent me to Bearss Academy, a small private school. A lot of white parents did this at that time and still do today. They didn't send me to the private school to get me away from black kids per se but did it because I wasn't getting an education. I was unhappy, angry, and unmotivated, and my grades certainly reflected this.

I didn't like the private school either, but for a different reason. The classes were small and all-white, but it was run in a strict, old-school way. The principal, Mr. Bearss, carried a paddle and wasn't shy about using it. He wore a big class ring on his hand, and if you acted up, he'd turn it upside down and hit you on the top of the head with it. Or he might jerk you out of your desk and wear you out with his paddle right there in front of everyone. These days he'd be arrested for that.

Though I still disliked school and hated being cooped up, I didn't hate Bearss as much as I'd hated Bailey. I also started getting an education. Because the classes were small, the teachers could see what I didn't know, which was a lot, and worked with me individually, making me stay after school and even holding me back a year. I can't say that I liked the teachers, but the harsh discipline was better than none at all.

Bearss only went through ninth grade, so I reentered the public high school as a sophomore. Murrah High School was about 65 percent black, and I didn't feel as isolated as I had at Bailey. It wasn't as chaotic and disorganized as Bailey was, either, but it was still racially divided and unofficially segregated. The races didn't mix socially; there were even separate proms. The parking lot behind the school was used almost exclusively by the white kids—the black kids who had cars parked in front or on the sides of the school.

There were a few turf fights over the unwritten laws from time to time. I heard about some of them but only saw one, and it was nothing much. Some black kid was mouthing off in the parking lot, and a white kid took him on; then others joined in. It broke up pretty quickly when a couple of coaches came outside and made them stop. No one got hurt or even suspended. As I recall, all of the "incidents" were like that. Overall, Murrah was fairly peaceful. There was just this simmering feeling, an underlying tension. You couldn't relax around people on the other side; you had to watch what you said and did, because if things went wrong, there would be trouble.

Perhaps Murrah was easier for me because I was older and had more freedom. In my case, this meant the freedom to skip school. I was never part of the in crowd, but I had a lot of friends, and many of them were like me—they hated school and liked raising hell. I wouldn't call myself the leader, although others did. We were all the independent sort.

Though my mother loved me very much, she grew increasingly frustrated with my behavior and her failure to find a way to bring me closer to the family. By the time I was in my midteens, my father was spending much of his time working out of state—in Alaska, New Mexico, and other places. And without his more dominant presence, I became increasingly rebellious. Despite her best efforts, my mother had less and less control over me, and I believe she pretty much gave up at some point. Though I didn't realize it at the time, I was now entering a wild and reckless stretch that would end badly.

A couple of close friends, Rick and Lick, were regular fishing, hunting, and drinking buddies. We also loved to go frog-gigging at night. We'd load up a boat with cold beer and paddle down creeks or lakes, gigging bullfrogs. Their legs are delicious—they really do taste like chicken. Often we would skip school and go duck hunting in the morning or squirrel hunting in the afternoon and then get cleaned up and go out partying and drinking at night.

I started going to bars when I was sixteen. We knew the bars where they'd serve us without any trouble, particularly the Dutch

Bar. The proprietor, Sid, knew we were underage but we all had fake IDs, and that was good enough for him.

One of my best drinking buddies in high school was Mart Lamar. Mart was a lot of fun and loved to fight—a real badass for sure. He had an old Volkswagen bug that became our hell-raising vehicle, and I believe the only reason we weren't involved in an alcohol-related accident was because it was just too slow. Mart's VW carried plenty of drunk teenagers and saw more than its share of sexual encounters. We drank a lot of beer and sometimes whiskey, usually Jack Daniels or Jim Beam. Sometimes we hung out at the Dutch Bar, but often we were out in the woods. Oddly, the sewage lagoons in North Jackson were a popular place to meet up at night and drink. I never had steady girlfriends, but I had plenty of girls as friends. I didn't "fall in love" like some of my friends. I liked to drink and party and didn't want to be tied down. I liked girls in the way all teenage boys like girls, and it had nothing to do with romance.

The closest I ever came to having a girlfriend in high school was Julie McMullin. Julie attended Jackson Prep and was very smart and pretty. I developed a crush on her and would have liked for it to have been more. I believe she had a crush on me, too, but there was no way it could ever develop into a relationship. Julie was a good student and had none of the wild traits that I did. She was killed in a car accident in 1978, and I was deeply saddened when I heard the news. At that point, I hadn't seen her in more than a year. I think of Julie often and have very fond memories of her.

People who knew me back then remember that I liked to mouth off, especially at blacks. Sometimes my friends joined me, and sometimes they'd just shrug and say, "There goes George." I've always found it pretty easy to talk people around to my point of view, maybe because I have a big voice, or maybe it sounds bigger than it is because I'm not a tall guy. In fact, I'm short. But I don't really remember starting trouble with blacks when I was in high school. Although I could be loud, I wasn't violent. I got along relatively well at Murrah and didn't socialize with blacks, so I had little opportunity to have run-ins with them.

I wasn't always in trouble. I never let my hell-raising or drinking interfere with work. My first real job, at age fifteen, was working residential construction for Ricky Turner and his father, Hozie. Along with some other kids, I worked after school and on weekends building houses in our neighborhood. Our duties were always unskilled, manual labor. The Turners, especially Hozie, demanded hard, high-quality work. He allowed us to go to the water keg twice in the morning and three times in the afternoon. The other rules were simple: if you didn't work hard and do a good job, you were fired. Ricky and Hozie were tough bosses, but they were fair. I learned what a good work ethic was, and it's a lesson I have carried with me throughout my life.

After that, I got a part-time job loading UPS trucks. I worked the evening shift and earned decent money. I was proud of how hard I worked and that I didn't count on my family to support me. When I got my first UPS paycheck, I immediately noticed that they had deducted union dues. I had not joined the union and had no intention of joining, so I figured the deduction was a mistake. I took my check stub to my boss and asked him to address the problem, and he told me that I had no choice but to join because membership was mandatory. When I objected, he referred me to his boss and the local union steward. I argued vociferously about being forced to join and pay dues, but to no avail. To this day, I am incredulous that workers can be forced to join a union against their will.

When I grew up, very few of us kids received spending money from our parents. My grandfather had been a prominent figure in Jackson—there were buildings all over the city that he'd designed—but I was taught that he'd worked for everything he had, that that's what men do. My dad never provided me with a car or gave me money. My first vehicle was a souped-up Jeep I bought after saving thirteen hundred dollars from my after-school jobs. It had no top and wasn't much fun to drive on cold, rainy days, but it was pure badass in the mud.

I still wasn't focused on school. I hated it and went as little as possible. I often referred to it as prison, a comparison that later made me shake my head at my own stupidity. Mostly what I hated about school was people I didn't respect trying to tell me what to do. It's not that I disliked all authority figures, just those who didn't deserve it, the kind of people who threw their weight around simply because they could.

My grades were mostly Ds and a few Fs, but I was good at goofing off and pulling pranks. Once I brought a four-foot-long king snake to school because I knew there were a lot of kids at Murrah who were scared of snakes—mostly the black city kids. I carried it in a small briefcase and let a couple of my friends in on the joke I was going to play in study hall. When we entered the classroom, we saw a bunch of black kids gathered in the back corner, shooting dice. I took the snake out of my briefcase and wound it around my arm as I made my way to the back of the room. It caused a bigger uproar than I thought it would, and I ended up getting suspended.

My favorite teacher was Mr. Hall, who taught American government and history. I didn't study in his class either, although I did become interested in politics. Years later, after I was arrested in New Orleans, a newspaper wrote a story about me and the reporter asked Mr. Hall for his opinion of me as a student. He called me a "bush-league Charles Manson," which stunned me. To this day, I don't know why he called me that. I was always friendly with Mr. Hall and felt that he was fond of me. The book *Bayou of Pigs* quotes him as saying that I was a racist, that I once walked into his classroom and declared, "This class is full of niggers." I never said anything like that. For one thing, Murrah was nearly 70 percent black, and if I'd said something like that, there would have been major repercussions. *Bayou of Pigs* also claimed that I'd been recruited into the Klan in high school, which was untrue. That didn't occur until I was in the US Navy. After I was arrested and sent to prison, many people who knew me either exaggerated stories or flat-out invented them. I never knew why they had to tell outlandish stories about me, because there were plenty of true ones that needed no exaggeration.

After I discovered an interest in politics, I became a George Wallace supporter and attended a rally when he was running in the 1976 Mississippi Democratic presidential primary. A group of us, including Julie McMullin, went to the Wallace rally. I liked Wallace's stance on segregation and was impressed with the courage it took for him to run even though he was paralyzed and in a wheelchair. I was sorry when Jimmy Carter received the nomination.

My political and social views solidified as I got older, and I became more racist. It's true that I was more of a leader than a follower, but I never tried to make other people do anything. I was no Manson. It's also true that I wasn't a quiet sort—when I thought something was wrong I said so, and I didn't much care whether or not people agreed with me.

As far as school, the final straw came in my junior year. I believe I was in English class, though I paid so little attention that the subject is vague. We were taking a test when I turned around in my seat to say something to the guy behind me, and the teacher—a black woman whose name I've forgotten—accused me of looking at his paper.

"You were cheating," she said.

"I was not cheating," I said loudly. I was mad—really mad. I had not been cheating. I never cheated.

"Yes, you were cheating," she said. The she told me I'd get an F on the test. I didn't care about the F, but I wasn't going to sit there and let her accuse me of something I didn't do. If I had looked at his paper, I would have admitted it because that test didn't matter to me.

I stood up from my desk and yelled at her as she continued accusing me, making a scene. The assistant principal, Mr. Mangum, pulled me out of class and into his office, where he again suspended me for three days.

My parents weren't happy about my suspension, but by this time they were used to it. My father sighed and told me that I couldn't do things like that, that it was possible to stand up for the truth without getting into a yelling match with my teacher. I didn't argue with him, but I didn't agree. I liked the Billy Jack method better.

Shortly after my three-day suspension, I decided I'd had enough. I couldn't take it any longer and told my parents I was dropping out.

They didn't like it, of course, but when my father saw that my mind was made up, he conceded. I wasn't getting much of an education anyhow; in fact, my grades were so bad that I might not have graduated. To make the best of a bad situation, he suggested I get my GED and join the military. He had served on a minesweeper, the USS *Hazard*, in World War II. "You might like the navy," he said. "Get out, travel to new places, learn some skills, and then see what you want to do with the rest of your life."

It might seem odd that the navy appealed to me, in light of my feelings about authority infringing on my independence, but it didn't seem odd to me. I wanted an authority I could respect, and I respected the military. I took the GED and passed easily. A few days after my eighteenth birthday, I enlisted in the US Navy and set off to see the world. I was too young to realize that wherever you go, you have to take yourself with you.

CHAPTER THREE

Wrong Turns

Military recruiting commercials were all over TV in the late 1970s. *Be Someone Special—Join the Navy; Join the Navy, See the World;* or my favorite: *The Navy—It's Not Just a Job, It's an Adventure.* They were very effective commercials—they certainly sold me—and my expectations were high when I enlisted. I expected the navy to be full of men committed to protecting America and our values. I felt a little like Lawrence of Arabia, a favorite movie of mine, off to right wrongs and make a name for myself. And boy did I make a name for myself.

Not surprisingly, I was somewhat disappointed. At the time, Jimmy Carter was president, the draft had ended, and the services were accepting a lower class of people; the navy would take pretty much anyone who'd enlist. As a result, morale was bad, drug use was much greater than I had ever encountered growing up, racial problems were not uncommon, and discipline was lax. It wasn't a good time to be in the service, or at least it appeared that way to me.

On October 2, 1977, I struck out for boot camp in Orlando, Florida. My father dropped me off at 5:00 a.m. at the processing center on South State Street in Jackson. I spent much of the day completing paperwork, but mostly I waited. There were almost twenty of us processing into the military that day—about half going into the army, a couple to the marines, and a handful to the navy. That evening a van took four of us naval recruits to the Jackson Municipal Airport, where we boarded a chartered civilian plane. There were already a dozen or so new recruits on board, and we took off right after dark, making a stop in Birmingham to pick up more before heading to Orlando. We had a great time on the flight, consuming beer and mixed drinks the entire way. We all were pretty wasted by the time we got to Orlando. I don't think any of us ever thought about what awaited us there, but when we stumbled off the plane at 1:00 a.m., we were greeted by four crusty petty officers who got in our faces and screamed at us for arriving drunk. They put us into formation and marched us onto a bus, and off we headed to the Orlando Naval Training Institute.

When we arrived, they marched us to the barracks. By this point, I had been up for almost twenty-four hours and was very tired. I was relieved when we were assigned bunks and badly wanted to crawl into mine for a few hours of sleep before reveille, but the navy had different ideas. We were given mops and buckets and had to swab the decks of our berthing area and the head. This went on for several hours until reveille sounded. Then it was off to the galley for breakfast, followed by a full day of processing. My adventure had begun.

Navy boot camp wasn't too bad compared to the marines or the army. I performed better than average and made it through without a problem. The only hitch I encountered was during our fifth week of training, Competition Week. We were pitted against the other divisions at the Naval Training Institute. Despite my short stature, I have always been a fast runner—one of the fastest in my division if not *the* fastest. I wasn't a distance runner, but I was a hell of a sprinter, so I was chosen to represent our division in short races.

There were severe thunderstorms that day, and lightning was striking everywhere. For safety reasons, they moved the sprints inside the gym where we would have only ten yards between the finish line and a cinder-block wall. My first race had maybe a dozen of us. At the halfway point, I was at the front, running neck and neck with a long-legged black guy. As we approached the finish line, he slowed a bit to avoid hitting the cinder-block wall too hard. Not me. I crossed the finish line at full speed, immediately threw on the brakes, and stuck my hands out in front of me as I crashed into the wall. When my palms hit, there was a loud *whop* and excruciating pain in both of my wrists. I was sent directly to the infirmary.

X-rays showed that I had broken both wrists. But I had won the race. The naval corpsman who put on the casts suggested that maybe I should have been a marine.

Following my recovery and graduation from boot camp, I was stationed with about two hundred other young men on the USS *Concord* (AFS-5), a combat stores ship out of Norfolk, Virginia. I went in unrated, meaning that I was assigned to Deck Division D1. I didn't attend an A school after boot camp, as most sailors do. I was having a hard time deciding what field I wanted to go into, so my recruiter convinced me to go in unrated so I could move around and try different jobs. It sounded great. What he didn't tell me was that unrated sailors got assigned to the deck division and were known as deck apes.

My first job was basically that of a janitor. When enlisted men first report to a ship, they're rotated around performing odd jobs, some of them nasty, like helping in the galley or cleaning the head. I spent thirty days assigned to clean the head, and I was one of the best at the job. Every morning following ship's muster, I scrubbed toilets, showers, sinks, and floors; I polished the chrome hardware until it shined. It was a disgusting, thankless job that I thoroughly disliked, but I did it to the very best of my ability.

After that, I went to work in Deck Division. Deck apes mostly chipped paint—a lot of paint. The salty air makes paint blister, and our job was to chip off the old paint; grind or sand the railings, bulkheads, and decks until they were smooth; and then repaint them. And then do it again and again. It was hard, mind-numbing work, but I took pride in doing a good job. I wanted to be the best paint-chipper on the *Concord*, and I'm pretty sure I was. I got very high marks on my evaluation. I also worked as a rigger on a crew that sent pallets of supplies to ships cruising alongside us, about

150 feet away. We did this with a system of large deck winches and cables. We worked twelve to fourteen hours a day, followed by a four-hour watch at night, and I was so tired that when we took our lunch hour I would go to the berthing area and sleep.

Despite the hard work and long hours, I didn't complain. Along with a few others in my division, I was known as an up-and-comer. I thought I might eventually train to be a gunner's mate.

I became good friends with another hardworking deck ape, a Native American from Arizona, Bryan Lewis. I was one of only a handful of guys on board from the Deep South, and he was the only one from Arizona, so we were both experiencing culture shock, thrown in mostly with guys from urban areas on the East Coast. Bryan was young, too—only a year older than I was—and also small in stature.

It didn't bother me that he wasn't white; we made a joke of it. I called him Redskin, and he called me Redneck. I learned that many Native Americans didn't much like blacks, either. About a third of the men on board were black, and although they mostly kept to themselves, there was sometimes tension between the races. Not all of the blacks were into drugs—some were good workers—but it seemed that most of the bad morale and problems on board resulted from the poor performance and bad attitudes of the blacks and drug-using whites. At first I tried to keep my opinions to myself or shared them only with guys I trusted, like Bryan.

In January 1978, the *Concord* departed Norfolk for a cruise in the Mediterranean. To a nineteen-year-old kid, this was the big time. When we pulled out of the Norfolk dock, I was excited in spite of the state of morale on board, but leaving the States didn't improve morale one bit—it actually seemed to make it worse. There was one problem after another.

Before we'd made it to the Mediterranean, we lost two levels of the refrigerated reefer hold, so we had to make an emergency stop at the naval station at Rota, Spain, to get them repaired. A month later, a package conveyor malfunctioned, and someone was nearly beheaded. (I recall the Naval Criminal Investigative Service [NCIS] coming on board to investigate). And then, the night before we arrived in Palermo, Sicily, a group of men broke into the disbursing office and stole more than forty thousand dollars. The ship was searched and searched again, but the money was never found.

When we departed Palermo, the NCIS assigned two agents to ride with us. NCIS eventually removed several sailors from the ship, and it was assumed that they were the thieves, but no one told us anything official. The sailors removed were poor workers—*skaters*, in naval terminology—whom I had pegged as drug abusers.

Finally, in Palma de Mallorca, a sailor tried to set the captain's office and the library on fire. Both fires were extinguished, but the arsonist had also set some life jackets ablaze in the forward part of the ship. That fire spread rapidly before being detected, burning for most of a day before we could extinguish it. I was assigned to a crew that was tasked with removing all combustible materials in the path of the fire; we formed bucket brigades and passed all sorts of materials out of the affected area. There were not enough oxygen breathing apparatuses for everyone, but that didn't matter to any of us. Even with no form of respiratory protection, we entered compartments thick with smoke and removed all of the combustible material we could find. I was treated for smoke inhalation but returned to work the following day. The forward third of the ship suffered extensive damage in the fire, forcing us to return to the States for repairs. NCIS agents again boarded the *Concord*.

They caught the arsonist a few nights later when he attempted to set a fire in the helo deck on the ship's fantail. He was a Filipino guy in my deck division, and I knew him fairly well. He was another drug user and skater. Deck Division had many people who, like me, were high school dropouts, so we had a larger percentage of sailors who tended to be underachievers and problematic, though there were also many outstanding sailors who performed their duties admirably and to the highest naval standards.

The navy lived up to its promise—I saw the world and had some adventures. My Mediterranean cruise hadn't been all bad. Liberty call in ports across Spain, Italy, and France had been a real experience for me. The USO sponsored many guided tours of famous places that sailors could go on at bargain prices, and a lot of guys took advantage of these opportunities, but not me. These seemed mundane and boring, and I preferred to take my liberty call in red-light districts. I spent virtually all my money on alcohol and women, with the exception of a few guns I bought at the naval base in Naples. I had a lot of fun but was relieved when we returned home.

In the summer of 1978, we limped into the Philadelphia Shipyard for repairs, and there my adventures really began. The shipyard was located in South Philly. A few of us soon discovered Packer's Go-Go, a nearby titty bar we began frequenting. After I got to know the bartenders and the girls, I was invited to stay after closing. They would usher the nonregulars out the door at closing and lock up and then the girls would crank it up a few notches. Sometimes they did things with longneck beer bottles that I'd never dreamed of before Packer's.

One night a group of us decided to skip Packer's to see a movie that was playing at a drive-in theater across the river in New Jersey. The movie was *Animal House*. Seven of us piled into a single cab pickup truck, owned by John Hickman from Franklinton, Louisiana, and loaded it down with Pabst Blue Ribbon beer and a few fifths of Jim Beam. We had a great time—actually, too great of a time.

I awoke the next morning with a terrible headache and found myself in the back of the truck, traveling down the interstate. I had no idea where we were. I sat up and noted three others in the back with me and the other three up front. John was pushing it pretty hard, running at more than eighty miles an hour. The guys in the back were all asleep, so I slid open the window.

"Where the hell are we?" I asked.

"North Carolina en route to Mississippi on the first leg of our road trip," John replied.

The events of the previous night started coming back to me. We had gotten pretty drunk while watching the movie and decided to follow the example of Bluto, Otter, and the other members of Delta Tau Chi and take our own road trip. At the end of the movie, we had all decided that we should head for Mississippi. *What the hell*, I thought. I was already AWOL, so I might as well make the best of it. I sat back and dug through our ice chest looking for something to drink. I had cotton mouth and desperately wanted a big glass of water; finding nothing in the ice chest other than beer, I chomped on a few cubes of ice and then popped the top on a PBR.

Our trip lasted ten days and took us through sixteen states. We rotated riding in the pickup's cab and bed. When it rained, those of us in the back made ponchos out of garbage bags.

We were in trouble, of course. We went to captain's mast before Captain Otto Will, where I acted as our spokesperson, immediately launching into a tirade about how we had done it out of protest: "Captain, we are the workers who carry the load for so many who simply skate and contribute very little. We work long hours, performing hard work, while many of our fellow sailors sit back and watch." I went on to talk about drug use and even tossed some of the blame onto our division officer, a weak ensign who had been commissioned right out of college. Captain Will apparently had some sympathy, since we got a light punishment: we were restricted to the ship for a few days. That was it.

Philadelphia turned out to be a turning point for me, and not just because of titty bars and road trips. Doug, the Grand Dragon of the Mississippi KKK, was originally from Philadelphia. I was happy to meet other people who agreed with me, as I was convinced that the problems on the *Concord* resulted in large part from the mixing of the races and the inferiority of black culture. In hindsight, I know that the ship had as many whites as blacks who were lazy and abused drugs and that many of the racial problems came from a combination of too much testosterone and radically different cultures

converging in cramped quarters. However, at the time, these experiences convinced me that the races should be kept separate.

One night, two white sailors had been out drinking at a local
bar and were walking back to the ship when they met up with
another sailor, Battle, who was black. The story went that the white
guys jumped him and beat him up. I don't know why. Battle wasn't
a bad guy—he wasn't a troublemaker or anything. The two white
guys made it back to the ship first and went to their bunks. A short
while later, Battle got to his berth and woke up five or six of his
black friends. By this time it was the dead of night, so most everyone was asleep belowdecks when Battle and his buddies pulled the
two white guys out of their bunks. It nearly turned into a major
brawl, but most of us felt that if Battle's story was accurate, the white
sailors who jumped him had it coming. Like I said, he wasn't a bad
guy, and I had no reason to believe he would make the story up.

Shortly after this incident, I came into contact with Doug. We
had a number of phone conversations. He spoke with a strong Yan-
kee accent, and I remember thinking it a bit odd that he was the
head of the Mississippi KKK. I don't remember how we made our
initial contact or the details of our talks except that he asked me to
meet him in Tupelo during my next leave.

Tupelo was in the national news during the spring and summer
of 1978. The black community there had organized boycotts of white
merchants to protest police brutality and job discrimination. The
boycott had inflamed parts of the white community, particularly
the KKK, which until then had been fairly quiet. Pretty soon, the
national media became involved, mainly due to the Klan's resur-
gence, and Klan members began walking the streets of Tupelo in full
regalia. It was small stuff at first, but the media blew it out of proportion. That's exactly what Doug wanted; that's why he was in Tupelo.
He gave some extemporaneous speeches in public places—standing
on the steps of the Tupelo police station, for example, surrounded by
reporters and a bunch of Klan members decked out in hoods and
robes and carrying weapons. It made for a dramatic show.

One night, after one of these Klan rallies, I met with Doug in person. I was home on leave and drove up from Jackson to meet him. I'd spoken with him the day before and had mentioned that I was about to shoot gars and catch snakes in the Pearl River swamps. Doug said he needed a few poisonous snakes and asked me to bring him any that I caught. He didn't explain why he needed snakes, and not surprisingly, I was suspicious of his motives. After we hung up, I thought about it for a while and decided that it must be some sort of test. Surely a Klan leader would not ask a stranger to bring him a few snakes for no reason.

The following night, I met Doug in a parking lot behind a dilapidated motel. We had an agreed-upon meeting time and he'd given me a description of his car. There were no streetlights in the area. The only light came from the motel rooms. My headlights illuminated a car that matched the description, and I observed two men sitting in the front seat. I parked directly next to the car and got out, leaving my vehicle running. The driver emerged, introduced himself as Doug, and told me to shut off my ignition and kill my headlights. The man sitting in the passenger side never said a word or got out of the car.

It was a hot and muggy summer night in Mississippi, and standing on an asphalt parking lot made it that much worse. I was sweating and nervous but was determined not to show it. Doug was actually pretty pleasant, which put me more at ease. We discussed racial ideologies and what was currently happening in Tupelo. He was curious about the navy and asked if I would consider forming a Klan unit aboard the ship. Doug was a slick guy, very persuasive, and after my experiences on the Mediterranean Cruise from Hell, I was ripe to listen to whatever he had to say.

We talked for about an hour when he finally asked, "Were you able to catch any snakes?" Without answering, I went to the trunk of my car and retrieved a small cooler. I opened the top and pulled out a burlap sack containing two cottonmouth water moccasins. "Be careful, I've got two poisonous ones in here," I said. What I didn't tell

Doug was that several hours earlier, I had placed the burlap sack in the cooler on top of a couple bags of ice, making the snakes sluggish.

I untied the string. It was too dark to see, so I opened my car door and used the interior light to peer inside. The moccasins were coiled and motionless from the freezing temperatures, but Doug didn't know that.

"See them?" I asked, when I had the sack rolled about halfway down. He sneaked a quick look, the moccasins neatly coiled and staring directly at him with their steely eyes. He jerked his head and quickly backed away. It was obvious he didn't want anything to do with the snakes, so I retied the sack and placed them back in the cooler and returned it to my trunk. I had passed the test in a rather dramatic way.

Doug administered an oath to make me an official Klan member. He encouraged me to form a chapter on the *Concord* and then wrote and signed a short note saying he had administered the oath of membership to me. He gave me the note along with the names and contact phone numbers of two Klansmen, Kenny and Bob, in the Jackson area.

On my trip home, I stopped at Cypress Swamp Rest Area, on the Natchez Trace, and released the snakes back into the wild.

The next day I contacted Bob and arranged to meet him at his home near Florence. He was not at all what I expected. Bob was a big, jovial man who was obviously well educated. In fact, he had previously been a schoolteacher. He spoke eloquently and passionately, at times getting so excited that his voice would rise and he would begin pacing the room and gritting his teeth as he spoke about the need for segregation and how blacks and Jews were destroying the country. I sized Bob up as a dedicated racist, committed to the ideals of the Klan but also without a violent bone in his body. After listening to him for a couple hours, a car pulled up out front and two more Klansmen, Kenny and Larry, arrived.

I pegged Kenny and Larry as stereotypical Kluxers, much more of what I had expected. Kenny was nice enough and relatively friendly, although he was initially distrustful of me. Larry, who had a handgun sticking out of his belt, was quiet and reserved. He didn't speak when we shook hands and barely made eye contact. He hardly spoke the entire three hours, sitting across the room and watching as Bob, Kenny, and I discussed our racial viewpoints.

When the meeting ended, we all walked outside to the blue four-door sedan that Larry owned. I shook hands with Bob and Kenny, but Larry opened the driver's side door—revealing several shotguns, rifles, and handguns in the backseat—and got in without any further acknowledgment of me.

I reflected on our meeting during my drive back to Jackson. It seemed surreal that I had just attended my first official Klan meeting. I was excited but also apprehensive, and I couldn't figure out where the apprehension was coming from. I felt as if Bob had immediately accepted me as one of them but that Kenny, though friendly, was distrustful and suspicious of me. And I had no idea what was going through Larry's mind: he had said less than a dozen words to me in three hours, all the while staring at me with his beady black eyes.

When I returned to the *Concord*, I told a couple of my closest buds that I wanted to meet with them after we got off duty that day. We left the shipyard, bought a case of Rolling Rock, and then drove to someplace in rural New Jersey where we stopped and started drinking. I informed them that I had joined the Klan while home on leave and was considering starting a unit aboard the *Concord*. They were interested, so we discussed Klan ideologies until we needed to make another beer run. We picked up a couple more six-packs before returning to Philly, and by the time we'd arrived back on base, they were ready to join.

I sought out guys who were highly regarded on the ship and who, like me, prided themselves on doing a good job. All of them were sick of the problems caused by drug use and lack of discipline. By early 1979 there were about twenty new Klansmen on the *Concord*. The unit was made up of sailors from across the country: California,

Oklahoma, Louisiana, New York, Mississippi, Indiana, and Massachusetts. All of us were white, of course—the other thing we had in common was our animosity toward and distrust of blacks. We blamed them for the racial problems on board. All of us also held right-wing political beliefs (pro–United States, anticommunist, antidrug).

Looking back, it seems strange to me that I felt this way, especially since I had worked side by side with blacks on the ship and never had a confrontation with any of them. In fact, I considered many of them good workers. There was one black guy, Foy, with whom I'd spent some time chipping paint. We had pleasant conversations, and he actually agreed with me on many issues. I liked Foy and considered him a friend.

I was effective at recruiting people to join the Klan because I was good at figuring out who to talk to—or, more importantly, who *not* to talk to. The *Concord* wasn't a giant aircraft carrier with thousands of people; everyone pretty much knew everyone else. I was careful. I didn't want to talk to anyone who would blab about our organization. The Klan is and always has been a covert operation and the navy wasn't going to put up with the possibility of violence, so we had to keep it quiet or risk being thrown into the brig.

I did, however, talk about my Klan activities with Bryan, my Indian buddy and the only nonwhite person I was close to. I showed him some of the leaflets and forms; he called them my "propaganda papers." I think Bryan mostly thought my Klan stuff was funny, though he did warn me that I was going to cause people to get hurt if I wasn't careful.

"What if all the blacks and whites kill each other?" he asked. "Then the only ones left will be the Orientals, and they'll take over the ship!" And he'd laugh.

I told him if the Klan knew I was talking to him, they might kill him. "But I know you won't say anything, Redskin," I said. "'Cause I like you, Redskin, and you're a good person."

God, we were so young.

In spite of my precautions, our secret didn't last long; I was naive to think it would. We were still dry-docked at the Philadelphia Naval Shipyard when one of our members was driving onto base and got pulled over by shore patrol. He had been drinking, so his car was searched. They found a stash of guns, including a .22 semiautomatic rifle, and a couple of pistols that we used for target shooting. They also found Klan paraphernalia, leaflets, and other literature, the kind of materials I had gotten from Doug and handed out to members to help with recruitment.

NCIS got involved right away. It wasn't so much the guns—in fact, they returned the guns—but the Klan literature that concerned them. The NCIS investigator was a junior agent, Dave Brant, and I got to know him pretty well. The guy who'd been pulled over was under a lot of pressure to explain, and I felt a responsibility as the leader to come forward and meet with Brant. After a number of talks, I seemed to convince him that we were not a violent group and weren't planning any Klan activities on board the *Concord*. Agent Brant, who had been with NCIS for only a year when I met him, eventually became the director in 1997.

But now the navy knew we were organized on the ship, and though they didn't force us to disband, we knew they were watching. Others were watching, too. When we returned to our home port in Norfolk to get ready for another cruise, we discovered that the media had gotten hold of the story. The Klan coupled with the navy made for good news, I guess, but as the media often does, they not only blew it out of proportion but also got some things wrong.

There were a few reports of racial incidents in the Norfolk and Virginia Beach areas at the time—cross burnings in Jewish neighborhoods, I believe—and the media conflated those incidents with the KKK group on our ship. This was completely untrue. We did nothing like that at all, on or off the ship. If we had, the navy would have broken us up for sure.

We were not always innocent, of course, particularly when alcohol was involved. My buddies and I liked going to bars, and the

Virginia Beach area had a number of them that catered to sailors. Norfolk also had a large black population, so there were a lot of black bars, too, as well as Filipino bars and redneck bars. We didn't always stick to the redneck bars, though, and when we showed up at the others, we didn't always keep our opinions to ourselves.

The night before the *Concord* was to leave for a Mediterranean cruise, a group of us went out for one last drunk to O'Hara's Disco by the Sea. Despite the name, this was not an Irish or a redneck bar—it was mixed—so there were whites, blacks, Hispanics, and Filipinos in there, and it was crowded. The six of us went in and began to drink. Across the room was a larger group of black sailors, and they were drinking just as much as we were. Nothing much went wrong inside, though some racial names were bandied back and forth, and I admit that my group started it. The black guys left the bar about five minutes before we did. The parking lot was surrounded by a fairly high chain-link fence, and we saw them on the other side, drinking and milling about. Someone yelled something and someone else yelled something else, and pretty soon we were all yelling back and forth.

The fact that there were twice as many of them as there were of us makes it even more stupid that we rushed the fence. A big fight broke out, of course. It was more than just fists. One of the blacks had a broken beer bottle and attacked me with it, slicing my neck open. Blood gushed. When the fight was over, two bystanders pressed towels to my neck and rushed me to the hospital. Another guy in my group was also cut up pretty badly by a bottle, and one of the black guys got hit in the eye with a belt buckle. There was blood everywhere.

We were all taken to the same emergency room, where we sat together nursing our wounds. We were done fighting by then and even managed to joke about what a sight we were and what a hell of a night it had been.

I went back to the ship with more than thirty stitches in my neck. The emergency room doctor said I had come "within a few centimeters" of receiving a fatal cut that would have severed my jugular vein. The next morning I was called into the captain's quarters, and even though I was all bandaged up, Captain Armstrong wasn't at all sorry for me. In fact, he was furious, and I didn't blame him one bit. He was relatively new on the ship, and it probably hadn't helped his standing with his superiors to have a Klan unit in operation. And now, on the very morning the ship was to leave for the Mediterranean, he had half a dozen men banged up in a race brawl.

The upshot of my meeting with Captain Armstrong was that he decided we were simply too much trouble. He had the core Klansmen—seven of us—pulled off the ship for good. We were immediately transferred and put into temporary housing on the base, and the *Concord* left without us. I stayed in temporary housing on the base for a few days before they told me what they were going to do with me: transferring me to the USS *Detroit*, a much larger ship. The *Detroit* was in the Mediterranean at the time, so a little over a week later they flew me to the naval base in Rota, Spain; from there, I'd be flown to Sigonella, Sicily, and then there taken to meet up with the *Detroit*.

I learned that the *Concord* was just about to arrive in Rota to take on fresh fruits and vegetables for resupply to other ships. I had belongings on board that I wanted, so while I was waiting to be transferred, I went down to the dock to meet the *Concord* when it pulled in. Captain Armstrong was stunned to see me—the last time he had seen me was in Norfolk as he was chewing my ass out, and now here I was, waiting for him.

He was mad as hell, and I assume he called the base commander, because the shore patrol picked me up and locked me in the brig. The next day, the NCIS questioned me before hustling me onto a plane and making sure I got on the *Detroit*. But after less than a week, the captain decided he didn't want me there, either. He had been briefed about the fight at Norfolk and the Klan issues and figured I'd be trouble. When he told me he was going to transfer me, I said I'd prefer shore duty and asked if it would be possible for me to go to Maine or Alaska, two places that had always appealed to me. He was in such a hurry to get rid of me that the *Detroit* detoured to Naples so I could be transferred.

As soon as we got there, the shore patrol picked me up and took me to an amphibious assault ship that was moored in Naples Harbor. I was placed in the brig for the night, and then the next morning, the shore patrol picked me up and drove me to Rome Airport, where I was handcuffed and escorted through the terminal and placed on a civilian flight to New York. That's where it really got odd. In New York, airport security was waiting for me when I got off the plane. They placed me in handcuffs again and took me to an office, where I waited until the shore patrol came to retrieve me. Shore patrol took me to a naval installation, where I spent the night. The next morning they picked me up, took me back to the airport, put me in handcuffs, and escorted me to my gate for the flight to Norfolk. I waited in an office nearby until my flight was called, and then they escorted me to the gate and removed the handcuffs. I walked onto the plane unescorted as the other passengers looked at me with puzzled expressions.

I had no idea what to expect when I got to Norfolk; all I had was my orders, which said to report to the Norfolk Naval Base. When I exited the plane, there was no one to meet me. I scrambled around and found a ride to the base, showing up with my orders in hand only to find that no one had any idea I was coming.

After some confusion, I was placed in temporary housing and assigned to Commander Service Squadron 2. About twenty people worked there, under the command of an admiral and Lieutenant Commander R. L. Glass. I reported every day for a month and did clerical work or whatever else they wanted while the navy tried to figure out what to do with me.

I got along well with everyone in the unit, especially Lieutenant Commander Glass, who was my direct superior. He had been well briefed on my Klan activities but did not seem to hold them against me. Unfortunately, a national tabloid got wind of the story about the navy ship with the Klan on board, and the whole media mess blew up again. The tabloid ran a two-page article, complete with a photo of me and the *Concord* along with some exaggerated information. A Norfolk newspaper picked up the story and ran it. I gave them an interview, which did not go over well with the navy. And then other newspapers, some as far away as Alaska, picked it up. According to my father, it made me instantly famous—or infamous—at home in Jackson.

The media attention increased the tension in the Norfolk area, of course, and had another consequence for me personally. The leaders of the national Klan read the papers, too, always on the lookout to increase membership. Imperial Wizard Bill Wilkinson got in touch with me through Doug. Wilkinson wanted to take advantage of what was going on in the Norfolk area by holding a rally there that coming fall. He recruited me as an adviser or intermediary for him because I knew the area and had contacts there. I agreed and started helping him coordinate communications and recommending locations I thought would work best.

And then a CBS News correspondent, Ike Pappas, requested an interview. He directed his request to the chief of naval operations at the Pentagon, and the request worked its way down to Lieutenant Commander Glass, who brought me into his office. He talked to me man to man, not like a superior to a subordinate.

"You are going to ruin your entire future if you continue down this path with the Klan. It's not too late to put it behind you and move on as a productive sailor," he said.

I listened to him because I could tell he sincerely had my best interests in mind and because I respected him. Besides that, I agreed with him. I sat there for a few moments and said, "Yes, Sir." I no longer wanted to pursue Klan activities in the navy and was willing to let it drop. I brought up Maine or Alaska again and asked if he thought I could get shore duty.

My orders showed up a day or so later. I was to go to the naval air station at Brunswick, Maine, a relatively small antisubmarine-warfare base. I hoped no one there had heard of me.

I think I would have liked Maine except I hadn't been there long before my naval records from the *Concord* caught up with me. The last review Captain Armstrong gave me had some low marks. His explanation included, "His low marks in both Military Behavior and Adaptability are a direct result of his non-compliance with the Navy's Equal Opportunity Program." According to a September 1979 message from the *Concord*, "Seaman Malvaney is an acknowledged leader and organizer of the KU KLUX KLAN. He admits to recruiting for that organization among Navy members. Though he carefully avoided any overt efforts aboard this ship, his association with the National Klan leadership resulted in adverse press coverage that embarrassed his shipmates."

My records came in on an insecure line where many personnel had access to them. Coupled with the article in the tabloid, it didn't take long for it to be known that a Klansman was now on the base, and it made some people nervous. There were a lot of black sailors in Maine, and the base commander was worried there might be trouble. I met with him and assured him that I was done with the Klan activities: I just wanted to do my job and finish my service. He treated me sympathetically but still felt that my presence was a distraction. There was an enlisted club on base where the men drank beer and got a little rowdy now and then, and he was afraid of the potential for violence.

We discussed my naval career and mutually decided that it would be best for all if I left the navy. I asked him for an honorable discharge, and he agreed. I was honorably discharged on New Year's Eve 1979 and couldn't wait to get home to Mississippi.

I was free again. Older, too. But wiser? Not so much.

CHAPTER FOUR

Dead End

I t was quite a homecoming. It seemed as though everyone knew who I was and what I'd been up to. Some, especially local Klan members, approved of me. Others, including most members of my family, were skeptical or downright disapproving. I didn't really enjoy the attention. Outside of my family, people wanted to use my minor celebrity status to further their own agendas, whatever those happened to be. Meanwhile, I was trying to figure out what kind of agenda *I* wanted to further.

I met back up with Bob, Kenny, and Larry shortly after I returned home. They were having a Klan meeting at Bob's house near Florence, the same place I had met them shortly after joining. About a dozen or so other Klansmen were there that night, and I was received relatively warmly by most. The publicity of my activities in the navy had preceded me and made me somewhat of a celebrity among them. But Larry was still difficult to read. He was heavily armed, as were several other Klansmen, and his beady black eyes seemed to follow me wherever I went, same as they had before. When the meeting was breaking up, however, Larry approached me and shook my hand. For a brief moment we made eye contact, and I knew I had passed his test.

I wasn't sure what I wanted to do with myself now that my stint in the navy was over. I went back to my old construction job with Ricky Turner and later was hired as a welder's helper in a steel fabrication plant. I rented a small place in Jackson and got in touch with some of my old buddies.

One night shortly after my arrival, I was drinking at a friend's house. He lived near my parents, and I decided to spend the night at their house. As I was driving there, I rolled through a stop sign only a block from my house and was pulled over by two black police officers in my driveway. My dog, a 120-pound Newfoundland I'd named Wallace after George Wallace, was there to greet us. He was a great dog and very protective of me. I was a little drunk, so I was kind of belligerent, and one thing led to another. I don't think I was belligerent because the officers were black. I'd had run-ins with white officers, too, and had acted similarly. I simply didn't like being told what to do and hated being accused of what I considered trivial matters.

I don't recall everything that happened that night, but I do remember that they pulled me out of my car and were going to arrest me. Wallace didn't like that, so he went after one of the officers, and the other one shot him. It didn't kill him; Wallace was tough.

Wallace and I ran into the house. My mother was the only one home and she came out of her bedroom to see what was going on. We heard the officers calling for backup, ordering me to come out of the house. Maybe I wouldn't have if I'd been alone, but my mother was upset, so I went into the yard. They tackled me, put me in handcuffs, and arrested me and charged me with two counts of assaulting police officers, resisting arrest, and disorderly conduct. I was later convicted and received fines and a suspended jail sentence. The convictions were eventually expunged from my record.

Despite this run-in, I was restless because everything seemed so tame. I missed the sense of adventure I'd had in the navy, and I missed the camaraderie and the feeling of doing something important that I got from my Klan activities on the *Concord*. The Klan in Mississippi in the early 1980s was fairly active, with ties to Klan organizations in other states. I welcomed their attention at first, because I believed in their cause and wanted to promote it. For about six to eight months, I threw myself into helping promote the Mississippi Klan's agenda.

Some newspaper accounts later insinuated that I'd attended paramilitary Klan camps in Alabama for a time, but that wasn't true. My role was mostly behind the scenes, organizing certain activities and working alongside active Klansman to make the organization more effective. For example, I coordinated with the Jackson Police Department when we held a rally on the steps of the Hinds County Courthouse to ensure that things stayed peaceful. I attended the rally but wasn't one of the speakers.

Besides coordinating activities, I tried to recruit more good and decent people into joining the Klan. My efforts were not organized recruiting but informal talks with folks around Jackson. I was looking for a higher class of citizen, like the ones I'd recruited in the navy.

I talked to some businesspeople, but mostly I concentrated on middle-class and blue-collar working people. They wanted to know what the Klan could do to change things like the excessive dependence on welfare and government interference. I talked with both men and women—family people who held jobs and didn't cause trouble, who tried to raise their kids right and keep them away from drugs. That is, they were average, everyday sorts of people. When we talked, I stayed away from anti-black rhetoric and simply explained the Klan's support for whites and segregation and emphasized working within the law, not violently against it.

I admired David Duke's approach to changing the Klan. He was trying to create a new base, a more professional Klansman. He didn't use racial slurs. In fact, he claimed that the Klan was not anti-black; instead, it was pro-white. He talked about southern heritage and Western family values, not about hatred or violence. Duke left the traditional Klan about this time because he couldn't stop members from doing what he called stupid and violent things.

After a brief honeymoon period, my relationship with my brothers in the local Klan deteriorated rapidly. It had been nothing like my previous experience. The Klansmen on the *Concord* were considered some of the best sailors on the ship. We took our jobs seriously and did them well and received high scores on our ratings. But *high class* did not apply to most of the members of the local Klan. There were a few good people and some smart people, but there were also a lot of ignorant ones. And they were not just ignorant but dumb, filled with hatred for whoever else they could blame for their own unhappy lives. Some were unemployed and living on welfare. They were sponges on society and represented exactly the things they claimed they were against—in spite of their antiwelfare rhetoric, they made no efforts to find jobs. The only difference between them and the blacks they attacked was the color of their skin.

They not only harbored ignorant opinions but did ignorant things, things that proved nothing and changed nothing, like burning crosses at a black newspaper and TV station. Because I've never been one to hide my opinions, it's not surprising that I quickly became very unpopular. The leadership wanted me gone. I realized that joining the Klan had been a foolish mistake, and it was time to disassociate myself from them for good. The local Klan later told the press that they kicked me out, but that's not accurate. It was a mutual decision. Disenchanted and disgusted, I moved on, and they were glad to see me go.

If I'd known I would end up branded a Klansman for the rest of my life, I might have taken a different path. But I didn't. And today I do not shirk the label. Though it's not something I'm proud of, I make no apologies for being a former Klansman. I own it. We are molded into the people we become not by life's pleasantries but by life's difficulties, adversity, and mistakes, and how we deal with them. I took my Klan experience and recognized it as a terrible mistake and became a better person as a result of it.

Even though I quit the Klan in 1980, I did not give up my associations with some former Klansmen and with others who wanted to achieve some of the same goals I did but with different tactics and a lot less ignorance.

One of those others was my Uncle Hollis, my mother's brother. He and I had always gotten along well, and I had a great deal of respect for him. He, too, had far-right views. During my time in the Jackson Klan, my mother asked him to "talk some sense into me," as she put it. She was afraid I'd get into big trouble. Uncle Hollis not only approved of my decision to quit the Klan but strongly encouraged it. "There are other ways of getting things done," he said. I knew he was right.

Two old friends of my father and grandfather, Sam Bowers and L. E. Matthews, contacted me, and in 1980 and 1981, I spent time with each of them. Both had been members of the Klan in the 1960s, though L. E. kept his involvement covert. (He was primarily a businessman who owned an electrical contracting company.) Sam was a student of world history and loved to pontificate on major uprisings or the mechanics of terrorism. I enjoyed listening to him. He had become infamous back in the 1960s when he formed a violent faction of the Klan, the White Knights of the Ku Klux Klan, and was alleged to have ordered the murders of civil rights workers James Chaney, Andrew Goodman, and Michael Schwerner in Neshoba County in 1964. Sam had ultimately been convicted of federal civil rights violations and had served time in federal prison in the 1970s. But these were not things he discussed with me, and I didn't bring them up because it was clear that certain lines were not to be crossed.

Sam's ideas differed from the "modern" Klan of the time. He didn't like organized meetings and marches and rallies. He felt that they were nothing more than events that allowed the Feds to take pictures and get tag numbers of vehicles. I can't speak for the Sam Bowers of the 1960s, but the Sam I came to know rarely, if ever, expounded racist viewpoints. I would describe the Sam Bowers of the 1980s as staunchly antigovernment and antiestablishment, much more of an extreme anarchist than a racist. He railed against the federal government and strongly supported many of the world's uprisings. Sam was an equal opportunity hater of whatever

government was in power and tended to support whoever was trying to take them down. He wasn't against violence, but thought it
should be narrowly targeted, done with a specific target and goal in
mind, and accomplished in secret and preferably at night.

Sam was not a stereotypical Klansman (or former Klansman) by
any stretch of the imagination. He was very intelligent and lived in
a black neighborhood in Laurel, Mississippi. I recall a conversation
with him after he had been to see *The Color Purple*, starring Whoopi
Goldberg and Danny Glover. He thoroughly enjoyed the movie and
loved Goldberg's performance. Sam described her acting skills as
"amazing." I found it ironic, though not too surprising, that one of
the only movies I ever heard Sam rave about had an uneducated
black girl struggling with racism and poverty as its protagonist. The
other movie that Sam loved was *Bonnie and Clyde*, starring Warren
Beatty and Faye Dunaway. He had an affinity for Bonnie and Clyde
and even wrote poetry about them. He romanticized their criminal
activities and thought of them as low-level revolutionaries fighting
a corrupt establishment.

Although I admired Sam and L. E., the person who had the most
influence on me at this time was a protégé of Sam's, Dannie Hawkins. Like Sam, Dannie had been a Klan warrior back in the 1960s,
although he was younger than both Sam and L. E. When I met Dannie, he was in his midthirties, about fifteen years older than I was.
He was also a clandestine warrior, keeping his activities as secret as
possible. Despite this, he had a hell of a reputation in the Jackson
area and was known to many, especially the police. A lot of policemen didn't like him, but most respected him, and everyone was
careful not to cross him. Although I didn't know it at the time, the
FBI suspected him of being involved in bombings and shootings as
well as being a Klan hitman.

Dannie had heard about me when I was in the navy, and we met
through mutual acquaintances when I got home. I liked him. He
was strong and passionate, and he put his beliefs into action. He had
fought for his ideals in the 1960s. He was loyal to those who were

loyal to him, and I admired him because of his integrity. I listened to him talk about what he'd done in the past and what he wanted to do in the future: many of his stories alluded to covert operations and great danger.

Then one day in the fall of 1980, Dannie showed that he wasn't done with adventuring. He and some other Klansmen had become involved in a plot chock-full of risk and high moral ideals. He invited me to participate.

I was young. I wanted adventure. I didn't want to listen to old stories—I wanted to make new ones. So I agreed to go along.

CHAPTER FIVE

High Adventure

I n 1980, while I was arguing with ignorant Klansmen, my new friend and mentor, Dannie Hawkins, was discussing a much bigger event. Some white supremacy groups were secretly planning to take over a small Caribbean country and install a right-wing, anti-Soviet government. I knew nothing about this at the time.

Dannie had been recruited by Mike Perdue, a former marine from Texas who had collaborated with members of pro-Aryan groups in the United States and Canada—including high-ups in the Klan, Don Black, and Wolfgang Droege—on a plan to overthrow the government of the tiny island of Dominica. They had first thought about taking over Grenada but decided that Dominica would make an easier target. It had been hit by a hurricane in 1979 and was having a variety of problems, including some caused by a Rastafarian group, the Dreads. Perdue and his coconspirators figured the government of the current prime minister, Eugenia Charles, was ripe for overthrow, and they planned to restore the former prime minister, Patrick John, to power. In return they would receive business concessions.

Perdue named his invasion plot Operation Red Dog. It is better known today by its satirical name, Bayou of Pigs.

In August 1980, Dannie Hawkins received a phone call from Perdue, who was then in Canada. Perdue explained the plan: they would charter a boat in New Orleans, load it with guns and ammunition, and rendezvous with Patrick John's people, including the

Dominican army, to stage the coup. Because of Dannie's extensive network of Klan contacts in the South, particularly in Mississippi, Perdue asked him to recruit a few trustworthy and reliable people to be a part of the invasion.

I was one of the first ones Dannie called. He was a smart man and could read people well, and he appealed to both my patriotism and my thirst for adventure. I was definitely interested—chiefly because I was bored, I think. Even so, I was hesitant at first. I liked to raise a little hell, and I was in favor of installing a government friendly to American interests, but I didn't want to commit until I had decided that the plan had a good chance of success.

I didn't fully sign on until Mike Perdue came down to Mississippi and Dannie arranged for the three of us to meet. We sat down at the restaurant at the Howard Johnson's Motor Lodge in South Jackson. It was late afternoon, and the restaurant was not very busy. Dannie and I arrived a few minutes early and chose a booth in a corner with no one sitting nearby. I ordered a glass of sweet tea as we waited on Perdue, and before long, a stocky middle-aged man approached the table.

We stood and exchanged the usual pleasantries as we shook hands. Then we settled into the booth and talked about my time in the navy. Perdue expounded on his own military exploits as a marine who'd served in Vietnam. I listened intently as he shifted the conversation toward the plot and who was in on it.

Perdue spoke confidently and convincingly. "It's going to be a success," he said. "I guarantee it."

He talked about Wolfgang, a shadowy German coconspirator who now lived in Canada, and a decorated Vietnam vet from North Carolina who would be part of the invasion force. He spoke of having spies in Dominica, actively gathering intelligence. The plan sounded wild, but it also appeared to be the real thing, not just ten white guys trying to overthrow the government of an all-black country. To me, the clincher was that Perdue said that several key players in Dominica were in on it—the former prime minister, former army officers and soldiers, and some revolutionaries. There was a great deal of support on the island, so I figured the plan might actually work.

Perdue painted the reason for the invasion as anticommunism. "We'll be helping to stop the spread of Cuban and Soviet influence in the Western Hemisphere," he said. This appealed to my sense of patriotism, since I was strongly pro-American and anti-Soviet, though I wasn't sure that Perdue was sincere about his motives. It sounded like a sales pitch to me, and I knew there had to be something else in it for him. I later heard many theories about his motives, including money laundering, a base for cocaine smuggling, and setting up a haven for white supremacists. I don't know if any of these were true, partly true, or false, but I was skeptical about the possibility of establishing a haven for white supremacists in a country inhabited by blacks.

Perdue also claimed that the CIA knew of the plan and was looking the other way. At this point, I considered backing out. I just didn't buy the idea that the CIA was supportive or even aware of the plot—that just didn't pass the smell test. I knew the plan was secret, dangerous, and illegal. But in my final analysis, the risk sold me. Risk equals adventure. It certainly wasn't the money—Perdue promised me three thousand dollars if the coup succeeded, and even in 1980, three thousand dollars wasn't much money for risking your life. But at twenty-one you don't really consider death as a possibility.

After Perdue finished his spiel, I asked him some questions that were pertinent to me: "When will the invasion take place?" "What type of weapons have you procured?" "What type of equipment are you procuring?" I queried him about Dominica's geography and population, the size of its police force, and how it was armed. He answered my questions knowledgeably and in detail.

The meeting lasted only about an hour, at which point Perdue asked, "So are you in or not?"

I looked him in the eye and said, "I'm in." Those two words set into motion a chain of events that drastically altered the course of my life, though not immediately.

For the next few weeks, not much happened. I assumed that Perdue and the rest of the team, none of whom I knew except for Dannie Hawkins, were busy arranging financing and finalizing invasion plans with the island contacts. Meanwhile, I tried to educate myself about Dominica. Until then, I hadn't even known the country existed. If the Internet had been around at the time, things would have been a lot easier, but in the early 1980s, all I had was the local library. I learned that it was a small island, only 290 square miles, with a population of no more than seventy thousand people. I read about the economy and the current government: some sources portrayed Eugenia Charles as a leftist with strong ties to Fidel Castro in Cuba.

Dannie was kept apprised of arrangements and the status of the plan, and he tried to keep me in the loop. He and Perdue talked on pay phones most of the time to avoid phone taps. I felt like I was in the middle of a spy thriller.

My role was to help obtain ammunition and guns. Perdue funneled money he got from financiers to Hawkins and me, and I used my network of Klan contacts in Mississippi and Alabama to locate sellers, procure the goods, and bring them back to Jackson.

I supplied plenty of firearms and ammunition. In all, I collected more than five thousand rounds of ammo and several assault rifles, most of them from Jackson and the surrounding areas. The weapons included .223-caliber assault rifles, 12-gauge riot shotguns, .45-caliber semiautomatic pistols, and a .44 magnum revolver. One weapon I even got from a Jackson police officer, Bennie Bennett, who was assigned to the Intelligence Division, which shadowed Klan activities.

I was also assigned the task of helping procure explosives. I traveled to Alabama and rendezvoused with a Klansman near Birmingham to obtain dynamite, detonating cord, and blasting caps. The dynamite came in boxes wrapped neatly in Christmas paper with little bows tied around them. When I returned from Alabama, I went straight to L. E. Matthews's house. (L. E. was one of the financiers of the plot.) He helped me unload the boxes, placing them on a patio table behind his house. We removed the wrapping and opened the packages to expose the sticks of dynamite, which were marked with traceable serial numbers that needed to be removed. L. E. went to his workshop and brought back an old metal toolbox, retrieving a set of nonferrous tools.

He instructed me to take one of the tools and begin carving the serial numbers out of each stick. While I did this, L. E. sat across the table from me, nonchalantly smoking a cigar. All the while, he was talking about his plans to grow sweet sorghum and make molasses from it using an old-fashioned press powered by mules or draft horses.

In all honesty, I was having a great time. I was neck-deep in a shadowy plot involving international intrigue, explosives, arms, secret meetings, and coded telephone calls, and I was loving it. I didn't give a lot of thought to what I expected to get out of my activities. I knew there was a chance of violence and bloodshed, so I kept a few guns for my own use, including an AR-180 semiautomatic assault rifle, but I can't say that this bothered me much. I didn't make plans for what I'd do after the invasion, figuring I'd stay in Dominica a while before returning home.

Although I enjoyed the secrecy and sense of high adventure, things weren't happening fast enough. I expected we'd be invading Dominica in late 1980, but that didn't happen. In January 1981, Hawkins got a call from Perdue saying that because of increased political strife on the island, he was postponing the plan until March. But in February the problems increased, and Eugenia Charles imprisoned Patrick John because she thought he was plotting to overthrow her. (She was right, of course.) Charles declared a state of emergency, and Perdue decided to postpone the invasion again, this time to late April. I started to wonder if it would ever happen.

I only knew about some of these problems at the time, and I knew nothing at all about the other issues Perdue was having with his own team. I learned later that the crew and boat captain who had been chartered to take us to Dominica, allegedly arranged by none other than David Duke, had backed out of the plan, and Perdue had had to scramble to get someone else. He approached Mike Howell, a Vietnam vet who had supposedly run guns to Nicaragua, and offered him twenty thousand dollars to take our "troops" to the island. That turned out to be a mistake.

Despite the problems, Perdue decided to go ahead with the plan. On the afternoon of April 25, 1981, I called my mother to tell her I'd gotten a job offshore and not to worry if she didn't see me for a while. Then Hawkins, an older guy named Bill who had been active in Klan circles in the 1960s, and I left Jackson in Hawkins's van to meet up with Mike Perdue and Wolfgang Droege, the high-ranking Canadian Klansman, in Baton Rouge. It was a cloudless Saturday and the atmosphere in the van felt celebratory, like we were going to an LSU football game.

Ten of us had dinner together that evening in the hotel restaurant. It was more of a social gathering since we couldn't discuss our business in public. This was the first time I had met five of my coconspirators. We were all sizing one another up, and I tried to get a sense of who I could depend on in a crisis situation—and, more important, who I could not depend on.

Droege was a rather odd guy. He was a friendly enough, but something about him gave me an uneasy feeling. Larry Jacklin was from Canada and a year older than I. He seemed okay but had a distinct Canadian accent that I found annoying. Mike Norris, from Alabama, had a serious demeanor to him and was obviously a very dedicated racist. Bob Prichard was a Vietnam veteran from North Carolina and seemed like a solid guy. I had reservations about Christopher, a big, barrel-chested man with a chiseled face and a flattop haircut. He definitely looked like a badass, but it seemed to me that he was trying too hard to come across as tough. My instincts were right: later on, when the Feds put the heat on him, he folded and told them everything.

Perdue had a large suite in the hotel, so that night and the following day, we had several meetings in his room to discuss our plan, which Perdue insisted on calling Operation Red Dog. I thought that was a corny name and referred to it simply as "the invasion plot." The meetings were all business: no one gave any speeches or tried to rally the troops. They were strictly operational planning sessions, making sure we all knew what was going to happen, where, and how we'd be doing our parts. No whys were needed at that point.

Perdue had brought along maps, photographs, world atlases, encyclopedias, and travel books, which we pored over. We memorized various important places, such as the island police station and other potential targets for takeover. We went through our equipment stores. We'd spent a lot of money on netting, mosquito repellent, gun-cleaning kits, and medical supplies, so we felt we were relatively well equipped.

The plan was to leave the next day from a Slidell marina outside of New Orleans, where Mike Howell's fifty-foot marine research boat was waiting for us. We'd load the boat with our weapons and embark on the ten-day trip to Dominica. There would be additional operational meetings on board to discuss details about what would happen when we arrived.

We planned to break up into groups in Dominica and rendezvous with local coconspirators and the remnants of the army. Our primary targets were the police station, the prime minister's palace, and the radio station; we knew there wouldn't be much opposition. Charles had already disbanded the army, so there was only the small police force. Perdue assured us that his other collaborators had been meeting with the local resistance and that they would assist us. There was a strange network of people involved in the coup. Droege had developed a relationship with the Rastafarian guerrillas, and they, too, were ready to help.

It later struck a lot of people as odd that the plan included a strong coalition between the KKK and various black groups such as the militant Rastafarians. The head of the Dominican army was black, and so was John. Some media reports after the invasion said that Perdue's goal was to set up a white supremacist state in Dominica, but to my knowledge, that isn't true.

I thought our plan was solid. I finally felt like Lawrence of Arabia. But neither I nor anyone else in our group knew that the invasion was doomed. According to most of the media reports that I read much later, Howell, the boat captain, turned us in. He'd taken Perdue's twenty grand and gone straight to the FBI. The FBI and ATF had been keeping Perdue under surveillance for the past several months; they'd also taped every meeting he'd had with Howell. To make matters worse, Perdue had given a "secret" interview to a reporter from a local radio station. The reporter went to the FBI, too.

They were waiting for us.

We left the hotel on the evening of Monday, April 27, in various vehicles carrying the ten of us and all our gear. We headed to where we'd arranged to rendezvous with Howell, a location near Slidell, Louisiana, not too far from the marina. Because he felt it would look suspicious for a caravan of vans and trucks to enter the marina, Howell brought two small moving trucks in which we could load our stash of equipment, weapons, and ammunition.

We spent an hour packing everything into one truck except for our handguns, a small amount of ammunition, and a Nazi flag brought by Droege; all of that stuff went into the second truck, which would carry us to the dock. The media made a big deal out of that flag later, but it was strictly a Droege thing, and I had no idea why he'd brought it along. Two undercover FBI agents masquerading as deckhands drove the trucks. The plan with the trucks had been cooked up by the FBI. It was pretty clever of them to separate us from most of our weapons; it cut down on the chance of violence, and today I'm glad they did.

We arrived at the gates of the marina. I heard them open, and we drove through. The truck stopped. It was pitch black and stuffy, and a feeling of reality was settling in. I was about to board a boat for a two-week trip to a Caribbean island to be part of an invasion force. Up until now it had been all talk and planning, but now it was real. No one said a word. My heart was racing.

I had wanted real adventure. I was about to get it.

PART TWO

George had an uncanny ability to instantly detect what kind of person he was dealing with and then tailor his approach to them, all while remaining honest.
—**Tom H.,** former convict and friend

CHAPTER SIX

Arresting the Dream

"You in the van. This is the FBI. You are under arrest." A loudspeaker does more than increase volume: it makes voices sound almost inhuman. No emotion—just big, very big. It's a cliché to say that my blood ran cold, but that's really what it felt like. My veins felt full of ice. It took longer for my mind to fully comprehend what was happening, but at that moment I knew it was over.

The loud, tinny voice repeated, "We are opening the van doors. Come out one at a time with your hands up."

The back door swung open. I could see nothing except for the blinding lights that shined directly into my eyes. Hands in the air, I faced a SWAT team of hard-faced men wearing black paramilitary uniforms and bulletproof vests with FBI stamped across their chests, automatic rifles trained right on me.

As soon as my feet hit the pavement, one of the agents grabbed me, pulled my hands behind my back, and handcuffed me. Another patted me down for weapons, and then each took one of my arms and they placed me in a waiting car. They got in after me. I saw my coconspirators being handled the same way, each of us in a separate vehicle. The car took off. I knew I was in a lot of trouble, but I'd learned to adapt quickly to situations. An agent read me my rights and told me I was being arrested for violation of the US Neutrality Act. I didn't know what that meant, but I nodded. I wasn't angry at the FBI; the agents were just doing their jobs. Oddly enough, I struck up a conversation with them. I don't recall what we talked about, but I do remember having what felt like a casual chat on the way to jail.

"We're taking you to jail in New Orleans," one of them informed me. His voice was matter-of-fact, like it was an everyday thing to him. Maybe it was. But from the time I heard the words *You in the van*, the experience felt totally surreal. This was not a minor arrest by county cops. This was the Feds.

It continued to feel surreal after we arrived at the Orleans Parish Community Correctional Center. They took my fingerprints and searched me again, then put me in a cell by myself. I was told that my arraignment would take place the next morning in federal court. After that, I actually fell asleep on my bunk. That's what you do when you're dreaming, isn't it?

Early the next morning, the US Marshals came to collect the coconspirators and take us to the Federal Courthouse for arraignment. They shackled us in leg irons and handcuffs and linked us together before herding us into their vans. Some news photographers were waiting in the parking lot, and one of them got a shot of us that appeared in the papers the next day. Some of us were grinning and looked as though were having a great time. I was at the front of the line, wearing a T-shirt advertising a bar, Bad Bob's. The photographer had caught me laughing at some joke a US Marshal had made, so I appear arrogant and tough. I look at that photograph today and it reminds me yet again not to believe everything you see in the media.

At the courthouse, we were all placed in a large holding cell, and an hour later we stood before the judge, where we were officially charged with violating the US Neutrality Act. That was the first time I understood which laws we had been breaking. I'd known that the invasion was shady and that we were breaking some laws, I just didn't know which ones.

Bail was set the same for all of us: $250,000. None of us had immediate access to that kind of money, so back we went to the holding cell. It was then that I was given my one phone call, which

I used to call someone I knew from my Klan days, Harry Kelley. Kelley was a prominent Jackson attorney who had defended Klansmen during the 1960s, and I had brought his business card with me, just in case. He took my call, but when I found out how much he charged, I knew I could never afford him. I'd have to take the court-appointed attorney instead.

No prison is a nice place, but for a local jail, the Orleans Community Correctional Center wasn't too bad. There were a lot of rough customers in for violent crimes, but the federal prisoners were segregated and tended to be a better lot.

I'd been assigned to a one-man cell, but during the day, prisoners were allowed to mix together in a central area. I learned a lot during the two months of my stay. I heard that dozens of prisoners were once left overnight in the prison parking lot because there was no place to put them. I heard stories of rapes, stabbings, and killings, but nothing like that occurred while I was there. Above all, I learned the three big lessons of prison life: (1) the food is likely to be awful (there, it was rice and beans every day); (2) never snitch or rat out another inmate; and (3) never show fear, because it will be seen as weakness. Prison is full of predators, and the weak are preyed on.

During the days, I mostly hung out with the guys from our invasion plot. I became pretty close to Bill. Bill had a dry sense of humor, and we kept each other's spirits up. We both agreed that the only way to deal with the situation we were in was to stay positive and upbeat. Getting down would only make things worse.

Dannie Hawkins, Don Black, and Mike Norris posted bond a few days after the arraignment, but the rest of us couldn't get out on bail. My parents, who might have been able to raise the 10 percent collateral or put up a property bond, refused to help me. They supported me by writing letters and visiting, but my father said I'd have to get out of this one myself. I didn't blame him for his decision—in fact, I agreed with it. I was responsible, and yet I wasn't sorry for what I had done. It was against the law, but I still thought it was right. I was sorry that the arrest put my family in a trying situation, though, and I felt particularly bad for my mother, who'd found out when a reporter called her the morning after my arrest to ask for a statement. My mother had no idea what was going on. At first she thought it was a tasteless joke, her son invading a foreign country. When the reporter convinced her it was true, she was hurt and scared, as any mother would be.

Over the next month, I had numerous meetings with my court-appointed attorney, Ralph Capitelli, who had worked out a deal with the US Attorney's Office under which I would plead guilty under the Federal Youth Corrections Act. Under the act (which was repealed in 1984), offenders under the age of twenty-six could receive sentences geared toward rehabilitation rather than punishment. I would receive a six-year sentence—four in prison and two out on parole. In addition, my felony conviction would be set aside and my civil liberties restored after I served my sentence and adhered to all parole requirements. If I went to trial and was convicted, I could get up to fifty years in prison, so this was not a bad deal, and Capitelli advised me to plead guilty.

In return, I had to cooperate with the interrogators from the FBI, ATF, and US Attorney's Office and disclose what I knew. Since my attorney had told the Feds I knew very little, I agreed. I was adamant that I would not rat out my fellow coconspirators who chose to go to trial.

During the following weeks, I was interrogated a number of times. It was clear that the government was primarily going after Dannie Hawkins and Don Black, who had pled not guilty and were going to trial. The officials were also very interested in L. E. Matthews's role in planning and financing the plot, though he was not yet under arrest. They'd been after him for some time because of his Klan activities in the 1960s, when he was allegedly a master bomb maker, and they saw this as an opportunity to finally nail him on a conspiracy or explosives charge. They asked few questions about Mike Perdue, and I later learned that Perdue was cooperating with the Feds and had given them detailed information about L. E.'s involvement. I also learned that Perdue's stories of being a marine in Vietnam and Nicaragua were just that—stories—and that he was secretly homosexual, which was anathema to the Klan. He was a con man, pure and simple, and a rat to boot.

Despite agreeing to cooperate, I did not tell my interrogators everything or give them anything of value against my coconspirators. My answers to the interrogators were all variations of *I don't know anything about L. E. I hardly know L. E. at all. He was a business acquaintance of my grandfather. I don't know where the money or explosives came from, and to my knowledge, L. E. had nothing to do with the plot.*

Back in my cell, I worried whether Dannie and L. E. thought I might flip—others besides Perdue had—so I wrote a letter to Dannie. I knew the Feds would read it before it was mailed, but I was betting that they'd written me off as a punk kid who wouldn't know he didn't have confidentiality.

I wrote that I was being asked all sorts of strange questions and didn't understand why they were asking me since I didn't know anything. I listed the questions—such as where the financing and the explosives had come from—and said I was answering them the best I could, but since I didn't know anything, I just kept saying, "I don't know." I knew that when Dannie got the letter, he'd tell L. E., and they'd know I was tight-lipped and was going to stay that way. And it would also help L. E. to know what questions the FBI and ATF were asking.

A few days before Dannie's trial began, my attorney entered my guilty plea and a sentencing date was set. I would soon find out whether the judge would accept my plea deal and where I would be serving my time. While I waited, I was called to testify at the trial of Hawkins, Black, and Norris.

I didn't testify for the prosecution—they had given up on me telling them anything of value. Instead, the defense called me to testify on Dannie's behalf. I said that I knew nothing about Dannie's involvement in acquiring weapons or explosives and that I had never seen him with a firearm of any kind—he was a convicted felon and could not legally possess a firearm. The prosecution was trying to prove that Perdue, Hawkins, and Black had been attempting to set up a black market cocaine operation in Dominica, and I testified that I knew nothing about that, either.

After being questioned by the defense attorneys, I was cross-examined by the assistant US attorney, Lindsay Larson. I noticed that he was holding my AR-180 semiautomatic assault rifle.

"Mr. Malvaney, is this your rifle?" he asked.

"No, Sir, it is not," I said.

Because I had previously admitted that the rifle was mine, Larson looked confused. He asked me again, and I again replied, "No, Sir, that is not my rifle."

By that time he was standing directly in front of me. I looked him straight in the eye and smirked as I said, "That *was* my rifle." The entire courtroom, including the jury, erupted into laughter. Even the judge, Lansing Mitchell, got a chuckle out of it. The only person who didn't laugh was Larson.

After Dannie's trial, the ATF and federal prosecutors tried one last time to get me to flip on L. E., who had since been arrested and charged with financing the plot. I could tell that Larson and the lead ATF agent, John Osberg, suspected me of lying or evasion and were frustrated because I wouldn't play ball with them. Osberg asked me flat out why I was protecting L. E. and Hawkins. Was I scared of them? Had they threatened me?

"I'm not protecting anyone," I said. "I told the truth and that's all I can do."

L. E. eventually went to trial and was acquitted on all charges related to the plot. Hawkins and Black were found guilty of conspiracy and violation of the Neutrality Act. But Norris, who like me was twenty-one and a Klansman, was found not guilty. The jury seemed to think he was ignorant of what was really going on, simply led astray by bad guys who'd taken advantage of him. They probably would have found me not guilty if I'd pled that way.

To this day, I'm proud that I didn't rat on Dannie, L. E., or anyone else involved in the Dominica invasion. Several of my coconspirators did roll over and testify for the prosecution, and I find this inexcusable. I have no respect for people who betray their friends or partners to save themselves. I believe you man up and take your punishment, and that's exactly what I did.

When the day of my sentencing finally came in early July, I was more than ready. I was eager to leave the Orleans Parish jail and get on with serving my sentence wherever I was sent. There's an old prison cliché, "If you can't do the time then don't do the crime." I was going to show everyone that I could do the time.

My parents; my sister, Lucienne; and a friend, Ken Williams, came to the sentencing in my support, which I appreciated. They sat in the back of the courtroom while the six of us who'd pled guilty were led before the judge, one by one. Judge Mitchell was again presiding. He sentenced the first four, all of whom were over twenty-six, to six years each in federal prison. Then he turned to Larry Jacklin and me, both of us twenty-one. He picked up a short stack of letters and said they were from some people in Jackson, including the chief of police and the adjutant general of the Mississippi National Guard, asking him to be lenient with me. He told me that because of my youth and the people who'd spoken up for me, he would sentence me under the Federal Youth Corrections Act, which meant four years instead of six.

"Don't make me sorry I gave you this break," he said.

I turned around and gave my parents and friends a thumbs up. Then my hands were cuffed and legs were shackled, and we were led out of the courtroom and taken back to the Orleans Parish jail to await transfer to a federal prison. A few days later, we were informed that Larry would be sent to Michigan and I would be going to Bastrop, Texas.

My family was allowed to visit to say good-bye. It was just like on television. We were separated by a wall of glass with a telephone on either side. The visit was not emotional. I was determined to remain positive, a trait I must have learned from my parents, because they maintained the same upbeat attitude. No one cried.

CHAPTER SEVEN

The Wake-Up Call

I had heard that federal prisons were nice places—"Club Fed" is a common description I hear today—but I soon learned that these descriptions are for the minimum-security prison camps, reserved primarily for white-collar criminals, and had no bearing on the medium- and maximum-security joints that I would soon experience.

"In transit," I left New Orleans on a prison van, en route to the federal prison in Bastrop. Or so I thought. Turns out "in transit" means something different to the US Bureau of Prisons, because I was first being sent to a federal prison in Tallahassee. Who but the federal government would send someone from Louisiana to Texas by way of Florida? I learned that this mode of transferring prisoners was common. At first I thought it was because the Feds were inefficient and disorganized, but I later came to believe that it was another way to keep convicts off balance and feeling helpless, like a herd of animals. Cows don't have to know where they're going or why, and neither did we.

It was dark, hot, and muggy when we finally arrived at Tallahassee Federal Correctional Institute. Miles and miles of razor wire and high chain-link fences surrounded the prison. It looked much different than the New Orleans jail—much more menacing. They hustled us off the bus and into the receiving area, where we were strip-searched, cavity-searched, given new clothes (tan pants, tan shirt, tan underwear), and marched off to the solitary confinement cell block, also known as the Hole, where they housed prisoners who were there for disciplinary reasons or in transit to other prisons.

I could feel the eyes of the other inmates following me as I passed their cells; a few of them stood gripping the bars. No one said a word.

Everything happened quickly, but it seemed like slow motion, as if I was moving underwater. The months after my arrest seemed dreamlike, too, and they are blurry in my memory. It was late when I finally sank down on a bunk in my new cell, eventually falling asleep even though it hurt to breathe the hot air.

I awoke covered in sweat, hearing someone calling "Cups up, cups up" coming down the corridor. I don't know why that phrase has stayed with me, but it has. Even after I learned that it meant coffee, to me it meant that I was now an inmate, a real prisoner in a real prison. I was no longer free. I could not go outside. The swamps and woods of Mississippi that I loved so much were only distant memories. This was my life for the next four years. I was twenty-two years old, and four years seemed like an eternity.

Acceptance had finally set in. So now what? I had never been a person who looked back—I'd always tried to look forward. Obviously, I had made some mistakes—big ones—or I wouldn't be sweating in this hellhole in Florida. Where had I gone wrong? What was I going to do with this experience? How could I learn from it? How could I make the best of it? How could I become a better person? I didn't know the answers to any of those questions yet, but at that moment, sitting on my sweat-drenched bunk with a cup of lukewarm coffee, I determined I would answer them and use the answers to improve my life.

The worst thing about Tallahassee was the heat. Outside in the shade, the temperature hovered around a hundred degrees. Inside it was worse, sometimes far hotter. There was no air-conditioning, open windows, or ventilation—not even fans. The humidity was brutal. Every bit of my body, even my earlobes, dripped with sweat. We were being stewed.

Each cell in the Hole housed two men, with a total of about twelve separated from the prison's general population. All of us were either disciplinary cases or those waiting to be transferred to our new "homes," and none of us knew how long that wait would be—I found that some prisoners had been waiting weeks. My celly was Larry Jacklin, who had been with me on the failed Dominican plot. Like me, he'd pled guilty and received a lesser sentence. Now he was waiting to be transferred to a prison in Michigan. Larry was a Canadian and had signed onto the mission for the main reason I had—a thirst for adventure. Unfortunately, he, unlike me, couldn't make himself see prison as part of that adventure.

I was glad Larry was there because it gave me someone to talk to, but Larry didn't share my determination to learn something from our situation. He was visibly depressed, although he didn't say much—usually one- or two-word responses to whatever comment I made. He spent his time lying on his bunk with an arm draped over his eyes. It was hard to watch. I understood that our situation wasn't a good one, but I was determined to make the best of whatever I could. I didn't want to spend the next four years languishing in self-pity and depression—I wasn't going to go down that path. I was not going to let prison beat me.

Larry didn't have much of a chance to infect me with his downer attitude, though, because on our second day, the guards came and got him. The last thing he said to me before they took him away was, "It's been a rip."

Still, I hated to see him go. I was really in solitary confinement now.

The cell block they had placed me in was on permanent lock-down, which meant the inmates spent twenty-three and a half hours a day in their cells. For half an hour, each man was allowed to walk up and down the corridor for "exercise." I learned about the realities of prison life on these walks by the other inmates' cells.

Solitary is boring, so when we got a chance, the inmates liked to talk. Most were friendly, a few that had a hardened presence to them, a presence that said, "Don't fuck with me." I rapidly learned prison lingo: a *hack* was a guard and a *piece* or a *shank* was a homemade knife. According to the prison veterans, shanks were crude but deadly.

Several cells down from me was Donnie, a violent guy and a veteran of the prison system who was serving a twenty-five year hitch for a string of bank robberies. He had served time in three federal prisons and one state joint. He was somewhat friendly, so when I was out of my cell for my daily half hour, I'd stop and talk. Donnie had been busted with a shank and sent to the Hole while awaiting a disciplinary hearing. He told me he'd been working in the maintenance shop and had gotten his hands on a spent welding rod. He had sharpened the tip by scraping it back and forth on a concrete sidewalk and then made a handle using the adhesive strips torn off of envelopes.

Donnie showed me a more peaceful skill: how to take the element out of a light bulb without breaking it and use the glass to boil water for tea or coffee. He also taught me how to get my hands on matches and tea bags by trading with other inmates or the orderlies. You become quite creative in prison.

In one of our conversations, he said, "Just do your bit and don't fuck with anyone. But if anyone fucks with you, then you need to fuck them up." He talked about the different federal prisons and warned me about one in particular, Atlanta, that he described as a "real shit hole and dangerous joint." I came to like Donnie even though he was a hardened criminal. I enjoyed my talks with him and appreciated his coaching on how to do time.

From Donnie and other prisoners I learned the difference between a "convict" and an "inmate." A convict doesn't fuck with anyone and doesn't like to be fucked with. If a convict sees a violent confrontation, he doesn't see a thing; he knows nothing. At the same time, he sees everything and keeps his mouth shut. And it's not just because he's afraid of reprisals. It's because society is different in prison. By contrast, an inmate sees and hears everything and tells what he knows. He is much more likely to get fucked. Nobody wants to be called an inmate; inmates are weak and can't be trusted, the lowest rung of prison society. I was going to be a convict.

Three times a week we received fresh sheets and a change of clothes, and we were allowed to take a shower during our half hour. Since it was so hot and everyone was so sweaty, the cell block smelled pretty ripe. After a day or two I went nose blind and stopped noticing the smell so much, although on shower days I briefly smelled all right, which made me notice how everyone else still stunk.

Tallahassee was heat, sweat, boredom, stagnant air, and more heat. Life there was ugly but not violent. I heard about shanks and how they were made, but I never saw one. I heard stories of killings and rapes in other prisons, but saw none of that or even heard of it. When you're in the Hole, like I was, nobody gets to mingle, so there's less opportunity for violence. Before I was arrested, I had pictured prison in a Hollywood way, but I didn't see that there. The gossip I heard as I walked down the cell block said I'd be exposed to it soon enough. I hoped they were wrong. They weren't.

Locked down and alone in my cell, I learned about myself from myself. There was nothing to do but lie on my bunk, sweat into the thin, stained mattress, and think.

I wrote to my parents, *I am locked in a seven-foot by ten-foot cell, twenty-four hours a day except half an hour to shower. It stays over 100 degrees in the daytime and not much cooler at night. We don't have anything to read, so all there is to do is lay around and sweat and look at the walls.*

But I was doing much more than laying around and sweating and looking at the walls. My mind was working overtime, evaluating myself almost as if I were evaluating someone else. I forced myself to objectively examine where I had gone so wrong that I landed in prison. Obviously, my participation in the planned invasion of Dominica brought me to that place, but the questions I asked myself were much deeper than that. I thought about my lifestyle, my beliefs, my friends, my choices, and the patterns that had led me astray. Solitary confinement provided an environment ripe for me to do some deep soul-searching.

I denied myself the solace of self-pity—I knew I had to take full responsibility for what I had done and especially what I'd said and thought. No one was to blame but me.

This wasn't easy to do, but it had a bright side; it meant that I was still in charge of my life. What I did, believed, and said, now and in the future, were also under my control. If I didn't want to return to prison, I had to change the things that weren't working. I wasn't going to make the same mistakes. But it was more than that—it was also about becoming a different person, a better person.

I had no idea where my life from this point would lead or how I would get there, but lying there in my bunk I was determined to find out. I was going to begin a transformation and get my life back on track. The question now was how I would do this. In the short time I'd been incarcerated, first in the New Orleans jail and then in federal prison, I had seen what happened to men who allowed themselves to wallow in anger—or worse, in depression. I remembered Larry and the defeat I'd seen on his face. I resolved that I was not going to let that happen to me. Yes, I hated prison, I hated not being free, but I didn't have to spend my time brooding about it. Instead of being angry or depressed, I reminded myself that four years was not forever. I chose to look at prison as an opportunity to change my life, an opportunity to better myself. It was still up to me. And there was another thing I held onto: according to convict gossip, the federal prison in Bastrop was new and modern, and it was air-conditioned. That fact alone made me feel encouraged.

I had been in Tallahassee a little over a week when a guard came to my cell one morning to tell me I was leaving. Finally headed to Bastrop, I thought, but my relief was short-lived. While I was being processed out, I learned that instead of Bastrop, I would temporarily be assigned to the US Penitentiary in Atlanta, precisely the place that Donnie had warned me about.

In Atlanta, a maximum-security prison said to be one of the worst in the United States, I learned the answers to the question of *how*.

CHAPTER EIGHT

Letters from Hell

I t was a drizzly July morning when the Bureau of Prisons van arrived at Atlanta Penitentiary with me on board. Through the bars on the van's window, I got my first sight of the prison, and a cold feeling came over me again. This penitentiary is old—one of the oldest in the country—and it looked it. It was almost gothic, like the witch's castle in *The Wizard of Oz*. Solid windowless walls with gun towers looming overhead, and big—so big it looked like it could swallow me whole.

Built in 1902, the Atlanta Penitentiary has housed many notorious convicts, including Al Capone. Atlanta has earned several dubious honors: the Fourth-Most-Notorious US Prison; one of the Fifty Craziest Prisons in the World for All Time; and one of the Twenty-Eight Most Dangerous Prisons in the US "Club Fed" it most definitely was not.

Atlanta was a "transfer prison" where convicts waited to be taken to their assigned locations, but some, most notably the Cuban refugees who had been housed there, had waited a long time. Many of the horror stories I'd heard were about those Cubans. They were part of the 1980 Mariel Boatlift, in which the United States had agreed to accept some refugees. But the Cubans in Atlanta were a special segment of this population; Castro had pulled a fast one by sending his country's most hardened prisoners as part of the group, forcing the United States to house these "undesirables." The worst of the worst were sent to Atlanta. When I arrived, the penitentiary was capable of housing about twenty-one hundred convicts, and two thousand of them were Cuban refugees. Some of them were criminally insane; all of them were angry.

Wearing leg shackles and handcuffs, I was marched out of the van and through the doors of this forbidding place into the receiving area. The standard exercise in humiliation—stripped naked, full body and cavity search—was performed by a poker-faced guard who looked under my tongue, down my throat, under my armpits and balls, in between my fingers and toes, and between my ass cheeks with my legs spread.

When I'd been thoroughly dehumanized, I was taken to my new "home," a one-man cell in D-house, also known as the Doghouse. As I was being escorted through the Doghouse it was clear that this was a much different prison than Tallahassee. Many of the convicts hanging out at the front of their cells were covered with prison tattoos, including on the face and head. Hard, expressionless eyes followed me as I walked by. The noise was lurid and intimidating— shrieking, screaming, and whistling filled the air. I thought, *Just what is this hellish place I'm walking into?*

When we got to my cell, the guard hollered to someone who remotely operated the door. It slid shut behind me, making an eerie clanging sound as it locked. I sat down on my bunk in a daze, trying to process what I was experiencing. I was having a difficult time wrapping my mind around my new environment, but I knew that this was one fucked-up place to be.

The Doghouse consisted of several hundred cells, back to back and four tiers high. Each cell had a bunk, a toilet, and a sink. The bottom tier was where the Americans were kept, with the top tiers reserved for Cubans. The American convicts were allowed out of our cells only three times a week, for one hour at a time, for showers and what was called exercise. Breakfast, lunch, and supper were brought to us.

The dominant color was a dim, solid gray, but there was nothing dim about the noise. The refugees above us constantly screamed at each other, even at night; there was a roar that never ceased. They were allowed to go to the chow hall for their meals, and during that time, the noise was even worse. It was not a wise time to sleep or linger near the bars at the front of the cell because the Cubans ran up and down our tier like wild animals, shrieking in Spanish. They'd sometimes spit at us, and their marksmanship was incredible. Or they'd fill a mop bucket with piss and shit and launch the contents as they ran past. The American cons warned me that Cubans might try to stab someone with a shank tied to the end of a mop or broomstick and that they targeted Americans who mouthed off to the Cuban orderlies or gave the Cuban prisoners a hard time in any way. There was no defense. Some of the Americans would cower in the back of their cells with their mattresses in front for protection.

I learned fast to keep my mouth shut, which was something I wasn't used to doing. There were a limited number of guards and a lot of angry Cubans, so the guards did little to help. They would stop any violence if they saw it happening, but they didn't much care about the mess or the noise. They left it up to the orderlies to deal with, and all of the orderlies were Cuban. The Cubans had the power to make my life miserable, so I didn't run my mouth. I had enough sense to know that when you're in the lion's den, you don't antagonize the lions.

Most of the orderlies weren't too bad, and if you didn't hassle them, they pretty much left you alone. But there was one orderly, Hector, who clearly hated Americans. He had a mean and aggressive demeanor that made me wary.

Hector was in his forties and spoke in a mixture of Spanish and English, enough that I could semicommunicate with him. When he was delivering our meals or pushing the book cart around, I met him at the cell bars. I sensed a side of Hector that could be violent and vindictive, so I treated him with respect but never showed any fear. Whenever I did approach him at the bars I always had a sharpened pencil behind my ear. It was the only weapon, however anemic, that I had in my possession. I had thought about what I would do if Hector ever turned violent: I would try to ram the sharpened pencil it into one of his eyes. Hector was never friendly with me and made it clear that he didn't like me (or any other American), but we established enough of a relationship that we were able to avoid any confrontation.

After two weeks in the Doghouse, I was moved to a different unit, AWB, which housed only Americans. I was placed in a six-man cell that already held seven convicts, all of them black.

My bunk consisted of a thin mattress, about two inches thick, on the concrete floor. It offered little comfort. Before I could get an actual bunk, I had to wait until the cons who had been there longer were shipped out. The rotation was one to two weeks, according to my cellmates. Even so, it was better than the Doghouse. That doesn't mean it was good. My seven cellmates were all from Washington, DC, and in prison for violent crimes. I think they all were murderers, even though they were young—in their late teens and early twenties.

I sat on my mattress and listened to them brag about how bad they were and what they had done. Some of them had been involved in crime since they were twelve, and all had been through the juvenile system, used and sold drugs, and committed multiple violent crimes. They were thugs, pure and simple, and they introduced me to a world I'd heard about but never seen.

Most were also largely illiterate—some completely so. I don't recall one of them who could read or write very well. I learned this my second night in AWB when I was lying on my mattress after lockdown, thinking about how the hell I had come to this godforsaken place.

I heard a shuffling sound close by and then a whisper. "Can you write me a letter?"

I sat up and looked at the guy on the floor next to me. He was hard to see in the dim light. Leon was very dark, his skin not brown but a real black; medium tall and husky, he looked tough, like they all did. He wasn't one of the boisterous ones, though. He hadn't said much since I'd been there.

"Yeah," I said. Leon had piqued my curiosity.

He handed me a pad of crumpled paper and a pencil (no pens allowed—they could be used as weapons). "It's for my mother," he said.

That's how it began, the most life-changing experience I had in prison and one of the most important of my entire life. For the next couple of weeks, I helped Leon write a letter every few nights. Most were for his mother, a few for his sister. They weren't easy to write. Leon had no education: from what he told me, he had never been to school because no one ever made him go. His vocabulary was so limited that it was almost like he couldn't speak. When he did speak, it was in a mumbling whisper. At first I tried to write down whatever he said and how he said it, but I quickly gave that up because it didn't make any sense. Leon didn't speak Mississippi and I didn't speak DC ghetto. Instead, I listened and paraphrased what I thought he was trying to get across. I had to listen to the feelings, the emotions behind the stumbling words.

It was evident from the first letter to his mother how much he loved and missed her, how he wanted to know that she was doing all right. He talked about his little sister and his worries that she would fall in with a bad crowd and end up in prison or prostitution. He begged his mother to take care of her, to make sure she went to school.

I read that first letter back to Leon when he finished talking. He didn't say much, but he nodded his head as I read, and even in the dim light I could see his face relax. "Yeah," he said when I finished. Then he went back to his bunk.

And this is how it went on those nights I wrote letters for Leon—I sort of became Leon, and while I did, my empathy for him grew. It was very important to me that I express his true sentiments and that his mother and sister know how he felt about them. It was a highlight for me as well as him when he received a response from his mother. Her letter made it clear not only that she was almost as uneducated as he was but also that she loved her son. I realized that they were destitute. They didn't own a car or have a telephone. They existed in a world of abject poverty. I began to feel real sorrow—not just for Leon but for his mother and sister, too.

I sweated over those letters because I came to like Leon. It was a surprise to me that I liked a murderous black thug, but I did. Just a year earlier, I had been an active member of the KKK, and now I was searching for the words to express a black murderer's feelings to his mother, and it meant a lot to me to get it right.

It wasn't long after I started writing letters for Leon that a couple of the other cons in my cell asked me to do the same for them. Like Leon, they'd wait until night because they didn't want to show weakness. Also like Leon, the things they wanted to say to their mothers, younger sisters and brothers, and grandmothers weren't much different than what I wrote in my own letters. I'd been thinking that my cellmates and others like them were horrible people without any good in them, but the letters showed me that the good was there—buried beneath lives fraught with poverty, lack of education and opportunity, and crime, but there.

I had been in AWB about a week when a con shipped out and a bunk became available. The unofficial protocol was for the senior con without a bunk to rotate to a top bunk. You would then wait your turn, based on seniority, for a bottom bunk to open up, at which point you would rotate to a bottom one. Another con sleeping on the concrete floor had been there longer, but the guys in the cell broke protocol and offered it to me. It was their way of repaying me for writing their letters. The black cons wanted to make a white southerner as comfortable as possible. The cliché that the pen is mightier than the sword seemed quite fitting to me: only my ability to read and write afforded me this luxury.

We began to share stories of our lives during the daytime, too. Our only common interest was sports, but we also enjoyed hearing the details of each other's lives back home. I learned about the inner city, and they learned about hunting and fishing in the woods and swamps. My cellies were intrigued with my stories of frog-gigging. They couldn't believe we would get into small boats at night and paddle around in swamps teeming with snakes and alligators just to gig frogs and eat them. Conversely, I couldn't believe their stories of life in the ghettos. It was almost like we came from different planets, and we found each other fascinating.

I was still an extreme racist at that point, yet there I was, surrounded by what could legitimately be called the dregs of society, and I found that those "dregs" had thoughts and feelings that were a lot like mine. They loved their mothers and sisters. They worried about their little brothers. They tried to share the hard lessons they'd learned. I started to see that there wasn't much difference between us except for the way we'd been raised. None of these guys had ever had a chance. Most of them were doomed to spend their lives in prison or die young.

Writing those letters, especially the ones for Leon, gave me my first emotional connection to a black person. I'd talked about airplanes with Jeffrey and chipped paint with Foy, but those were surface connections. Leon made it personal. I'd never felt sorry for anyone black before, and I began to think that I had been at least partially wrong. I began to have confusing and conflicting feelings about my racial beliefs. I tried to push those feelings aside and cling tightly to my staunch anti-black beliefs, but my doubts kept returning. It was the beginning of change, though I didn't realize it until much later.

Of course, not all my interactions with blacks were good ones. Although the nights when I wrote letters for my cellies were encouraging, the days were full of restlessness and uncertainty. I was surrounded by some very tough cons and never felt at ease.

I had been in AWB nearly two weeks when a half-page article was published in an Atlanta newspaper about the attempted invasion of Dominica that the press was calling the Bayou of Pigs. The article included my name and identified me as a Klansman.

In the common area, the convicts in my tier were discussing the article with the black guards, who only periodically entered AWB. My cellies didn't say much, and the few who did just seemed curious.

We'd come to know a little about each other and had developed not exactly friendships but fairly respectful relationships. They weren't surprised about my Klan affiliation: they knew I was from the South and I was white, so maybe they thought all southern white people were in the Klan. But to the guys in the other cells, I guess my past came as a shock and perhaps a threat.

The day after the article appeared, we were out of our cells when the first hostile reaction occurred. About fifteen or twenty of us were milling around, and only two were white. A black guy known as Shorty approached me. I'd watched him arrive in AWB just the previous day—he was a loud talker, was boisterous, and liked to make a big deal out of how tough he was.

Shorty got right in my face and raised his voice: "Look here, we got us a Klansman."

I heard a low rumble come from the group behind him, every one of them another bad case from DC. Most had entered the federal prison system directly from Lorton Reformatory, too hardened and high risk for them to handle.

I knew I had to do something and do it fast. If I made excuses or showed any weakness, they would kill me. I couldn't apologize for being a Klansman or try to wriggle out of it by saying I was an ex-Klansman.

"Yeah, that's right, I am," I said. I looked directly into Shorty's face, his mean eyes and angry snarl, the Muslim skullcap on his head. The cap gave me an idea. Shorty was a proud Muslim—he made sure everybody knew—and that meant he probably didn't like Jews. "I'm proud to be a Klansman, standing up for my race, just like you black Muslims stand up for the blacks," I said. "Neither one of us is gonna be a pawn for the Jews." I went on like this for a few minutes—how I admired the blacks for being proud of their race, hated the Jews because they dared to try to run things, plus a bunch of other stuff I also didn't really believe.

Shorty's face changed as he listened. When I finished, he said, "You are a wise man."

Now, I had never had a thing against the Jews. I had Jewish friends, and the anti-Semitism of the Klan was one of the things I never agreed with, but Shorty didn't know that. Much of the tension in the unit instantly evaporated as we continued our conversation about racial pride and the Jewish problem. I had dodged a bullet, at least temporarily. Though I'd gained Shorty's respect, I wasn't sure about the others. My black cellies were in my corner—in fact, I'd heard some of them defending me when Shorty started in—but there were others who still seemed angry, particularly a guy named Goggins. I would have to watch out for him.

The next day at lunch in the chow line, I found I was right. Goggins came up to me and said, "I'll get you, Klansman," or something like that. I ignored him. There were guards around, so I was fairly sure he wouldn't try anything right then, but I was also sure he would try again later.

That afternoon our cell block was allowed to watch a movie, *The Elephant Man*, in the auditorium. Things like that didn't happen often, so it was a big deal. I sat in the front row of the balcony with the other white convicts, while the blacks sat in the rows behind us. Then one of the black cons moved to the front row and sat next to me, immediately to my right. It was Goggins.

"I'm gonna shank you, motherfucker," he said.

I didn't know if he had a shank on him right then, so I tried to ignore him. He kept running his mouth, saying he was going to shank me, calling me a motherfucker and a Klansman, telling me I was going to die today. I started wondering if he really did have a weapon on him—it was possible, and I knew that if I just sat there and took his shit I would be labeled weak, which could mean a lot of bad things once we got back to AWB—not just being shanked but being raped. I was young, white, and small of stature, so I was a good target for sex pressure, and I wasn't going to be anyone's bitch. I would die first.

He reached over and grabbed my arm.

I remembered Donnie telling me, "If anyone fucks with you then you need to fuck them up." I thought about the prison saying,

"You do what you have to do." I knew I had to act, regardless of the consequences.

"Get your fucking hand off me," I said loudly.

"You ain't gonna do shit," he said.

That's when I lost it. Almost by reflex I jumped up and grabbed him by the neck. Everything happened fast after that. There were several guards in the balcony, and the one nearest us rushed in and pulled Goggins back, and with the help of other guards he knocked me down. The guards had hit the panic buttons on their radios, which alerted the Goon Squad, and a herd of them quickly rolled in decked out in riot gear. They dragged me away and left Goggins sitting there, not hurt at all. They thought I was the one who'd started it. I was an ex-Klansman, after all.

Within the hour, I was back in the Doghouse.

What I saw over the next month convinced me that many of the Cubans incarcerated there were not human beings. Some were nothing short of vermin—stabbings, beatings, and self-mutilations occurred; I heard one case of a self-castration. They were constantly attempting to light fires, flood the tiers, and destroy anything they could get their hands on, even the fans that were for their own comfort. I was told that before the Cubans came to Atlanta, the prison had a large population of pigeons and cats that the American convicts had raised as pets. When the Cubans arrived, the animals disappeared; the Cubans had caught and eaten them. And you didn't dare eat the bread they brought with your meals. It was baked in the prison bakery and the Americans swore that the Cuban cooks fucked the raw dough to get off. I never knew if this was true or not, but I didn't touch the bread.

I heard many stories about the craziness of Atlanta. Sometimes you didn't know what was fact and what was fiction, but one thing was certain: the Atlanta Penitentiary had damn sure earned its reputation as one hell of a crazy and dangerous place. In fact, in 1987, five years after my stay there, the Cubans rioted and partially took over much of it. When it was over, one refugee was dead, and many more were injured.

The Doghouse had a small fenced-in area that could almost be counted as "outside," where the Americans were taken three times a week for thirty minutes. You could see the sun and talk to other convicts. That was the extent of my social contact unless you count the Cuban orderlies. Otherwise, it was solitary confinement in my one-man cell. When the Cubans were screaming, it was too loud to talk to anyone anyway.

I was polite to the orderlies despite their unfriendliness. I tried to keep on their good side because they were the source of my one luxury—books. They wheeled a cart past our cells every so often, and if I was lucky, I could get a book. They were pretty beat-up. Most had no covers, and they were often missing chapters, but I'd read anything to cut the boredom, no matter the subject. One time I got lucky and received a mostly whole copy of Stephen King's *The Stand*, which was doubly great because it's not only a good book but a long one.

Little, however, interrupted the loneliness and boredom.

For a week or so, I was lucky to have a guy in the cell to my left who liked to talk. Gene was serving time for counterfeiting, and he was a staunch anarchist who didn't believe in any government at all and wanted to live by survival of the fittest.

Gene was older, maybe in his midsixties. He was interested in my experiences and viewed me as a revolutionary for my role in the Bayou of Pigs. We had many great conversations, standing at the bars at the front of our cells with me against the steel wall on my left and Gene on his right and talking into the corridor.

Gene was an animated guy who moved his hands a lot while he spoke. We could hear but not see each other, and after a few conversations I began to notice that I was subconsciously focusing my eyes on his shadow, which was cast by the ceiling light in our cells onto the gray floor in front of us. I would watch the movement of his hands, and when he wasn't animating with them, I focused on the face of his shadow as if I was looking into his eyes as he talked. When Gene moved away from the right wall, my eyes would follow. I got so I could tell his feelings.

After a couple days of talking, we developed a habit of meeting at the bars every morning to drink our coffee. One morning we were discussing a topic near and dear to both of us—gun control. Actually, we were having a lighthearted argument about guns and convicted felons being able to possess them.

"Government has no right to dictate who can or cannot own guns," he said.

"I disagree with you, Gene. Would you want these Cubans loose in society packing guns around your family?" I argued.

"The government has no right to restrict gun ownership," he hollered. His response was so passionate and animated that I saw the hand that was holding his coffee cup go straight up in the air. A moment later I watched as his coffee splattered onto the concrete floor in front of his cell. Something about actually seeing the coffee gave me an odd but real physical connection. For a few moments I stared at it, watching it slowly move a few inches before coming to a stop. This was an emotional moment for me: it was as if Gene was actually standing in front of me and we were having a normal conversation.

"Talking to shadows," as I later came to call it, made me realize just how lonely I'd become.

After Gene left the Doghouse, I had more days and weeks of nothing. Day after day of sitting in my cell with no company, nothing to do, little to read, and loud Spanish curses ringing in my ears. Eventually I trained myself to tune out the noise and tried to sleep as much as twelve or even fourteen restless hours a day. That still left ten to twelve hours of sheer boredom, but I didn't give in to dark thoughts. I just didn't let them into my consciousness. I continued to reflect on my past and plan for my future, and I continued to think about Leon, his mother, and his sister. Something had happened when I was writing his letters and reading his mother's letter to him.

The day after Gene transferred out, they placed another con in his cell. I don't recall his name, but he was a real special case. Sometimes he would talk almost nonstop to himself. He had assaulted a guard at a prison out west and was in transit to the federal prison hospital at Springfield, Missouri. I never really got into any significant conversations with him, but I did sometimes pass the time by standing at the bars adjacent to his cell and listening to him talk to himself. His "conversations" were usually incoherent ramblings. I was beginning to feel like a real-life character in a maximum-security version of *One Flew over the Cuckoo's Nest*.

I was really lonely at that point and missed Gene's camaraderie. With no one to talk to and almost nothing to read, I spent hour after hour and day after day lying in my bunk and thinking. I continued to try to figure out what had gotten me to this place. I knew I was going to get out one day, and I wanted to be ready. I was going to take this terrible experience and use it to change my life. And when I walked out of prison, I would not look back. I would not have to keep reflecting on the past.

Early one Thursday morning, a unit guard came to my cell and said, "Get dressed and roll up your mattress." It was one of the best things anyone had ever said to me. It meant I was leaving Atlanta at last. I felt as though I was hitting the streets a free man, not just going to another prison.

As I was being processed at receiving and discharge (R&D), I couldn't believe I was really leaving until my name was called and I was on the US Marshals' van. *Texas here I come*, I thought.

Most convicts stayed in Atlanta only a short time—two or three weeks at most. I was there for about two months. My friends and family speculated that I might have been held there as retribution for my Klan membership or because I'd refused to cooperate and rat on Dannie and L. E. The Klan is not popular with the Feds. I found out later that some high-level government people in Mississippi went to bat for me to get me moved out of Atlanta. June Walton, a staffer in Senator Thad Cochran's office, had pressured the Bureau of Prisons to move me out of Atlanta. I never met June, but I am thankful to her even now.

Maybe I was in Atlanta for so long as some kind of retribution or conspiracy, maybe not. I never found out, and it doesn't really matter. Despite being locked down in solitary confinement and experiencing some pretty miserable times, I had remained upbeat and positive about my future. I left Atlanta Penitentiary a stronger and better person than I was when I'd arrived. It was there that I'd begun to change.

CHAPTER NINE

Riding the Prison Buses

Before getting into the US Marshals' van, I was once again stripped and cavity-searched, and then I was handcuffed with my legs shackled. The handcuffs had a chain attached to them that ran through the belt loops on my pants, with only one foot of loose chain between my waist and hands. At least they weren't behind my back, but even so I couldn't lift my hands very high. This made using the bathroom practically impossible. I hoped it wouldn't take long to get to Texas.

There were ten of us in the van, none of whom I knew. We were transported to Charlie Brown Airfield in Atlanta, where we boarded an old prop-job airplane that belonged to the Bureau of Prisons. Many years later, when I watched the movie *Con Air*, I was reminded of flying on that transport plane.

After I was in my seat, we were told that we would arrive that evening in Oklahoma City; then we'd go by bus to a federal prison in El Reno. I knew this meant more time in solitary confinement. The marshals gave us no further information. When would I leave Oklahoma for Texas? No answer. Why did it take so long to fly from Georgia to Oklahoma? They answered that question by stopping in Terre Haute, Indiana, and again in Springfield, Missouri, where more prisoners were picked up and others discharged. When I fly today, I often hear people complain about being uncomfortable, and sometimes I think, *You should try it with leg shackles and handcuffs.*

I felt more like an animal than ever.

It was nearly dark when we landed at the Will Rogers Airport in Oklahoma City. From there I was loaded onto a prison bus and transported to El Reno Federal Correctional Institution. By now the routine was really old. Each time I arrived or departed from a prison, I was taken to R&D, where I was photographed, strip-searched, cavity-checked, and questioned. Strip searches and cavity checks are ostensibly done for security reasons, but there is no doubt they play an important role in accomplishing one of the prison administration's primary goals: intimidation and dehumanization.

The El Reno guards at R&D were friendly, to my surprise. They knew what I was in for and were curious—I was the first convict they'd ever encountered who had tried to overthrow a foreign government. They evidently found it more interesting than "normal" crimes like murder, bank robbery, drug smuggling, and kidnapping. They asked a lot of questions. By the time R&D was over, we were laughing.

I was placed in a cell on the second floor with a convict I'd met on the flight. He had done time at Bastrop, so I had him give me a rundown of the joint. The more he told me, the more I wanted to get there. He said it was a new joint, good food, and most important to me, there was air-conditioning. I was so tired of being "temporarily" in transit—temporary, my ass. I was also restless because of all the idle time I'd spent in the Hole in Tallahassee and Atlanta. All I wanted was to get to my destination, settle in, do whatever job they assigned me, and keep a low profile until my release date. I wanted to meet up with Bill, who I'd heard was in Bastrop, just to see a familiar face. I wanted to walk in a compound without handcuffs or leg shackles and not sit locked in a cell all day, every day, sweating like a pig. Eat in a cafeteria. Be in an outside prison yard where I could see the sun. I wanted to enjoy one small taste of freedom.

At least El Reno was an improvement over Atlanta. The best part was the absence of noise. No shrieking, screaming, or moaning; no Spanish curses echoing off the walls. All of the cons in my range wanted to do "easy time," and the best way to do that was through peace and quiet. And the Okie guards in El Reno didn't take any shit, so most cons tended to behave.

We were allowed out of our cells to go to the recreation yard three times a week. About twenty feet square, the yard was surrounded by twelve-foot fences and coil after coil of razor wire. It reminded me of a high-security dog kennel. But you could see the sky.

After a couple days at El Reno, a guard asked if I wanted to be the range orderly. I jumped at the chance. Being an orderly was great; it meant I could stay out of my cell most of the day. I pushed a broom or a mop up and down the cell-block corridors. I pushed the food and beverage cart, delivering meals and picking up empty trays. It might not sound like much to those who've never been imprisoned—in fact, it might sound like a filthy chore no one would want—but everything in life is relative. After nearly three months of stifling boredom, locked down in the Hole with very little to read, no one to talk to, just hours and hours of lying on a bunk sweating and thinking—well, being a range orderly still ranks as one of the best honors I was ever given.

Being an orderly also gave me some special fringe benefits. Besides pushing the meal cart, I also got to push the book cart around, and this meant I got first pick. When other cons returned a book, I kept it for myself if it looked interesting. I hadn't been much of a reader before I went to prison, but in prison I read everything I could get my hands on. Then there was hooch. On my first day of orderly duty, one con, Buff, called me over to the bars of his cell. Buff had been thrown in the Hole for fighting and had been given a month for punishment.

"If you can collect extra sugar and fruit from the food trays and give them to me, I'll cut you in on a batch of hooch I'm gonna make," he said.

I agreed. It had been a long time since I'd had a real drink.

Hooch is a homemade alcoholic drink, and alcohol is not permitted in prison—for obvious reasons. Cons make hooch from yeast, sugar, water, and fruit—typically grapefruit and oranges.

Over the next three days, I collected all of the ingredients Buff had requested. The sugar and grapefruit were easy. Most of the cons liked sugar in their coffee, so I had access to it on the cart. Grapefruit and oranges were often served for breakfast, and even if they were eaten, some of the pulp was usually left. The hard part was the yeast. The prison bakery used yeast, so I made friends with the orderlies who picked up the trays from the kitchen and talked them into getting me some.

"It's for Buff," I said. Buff was highly thought of among the El Reno population.

After I gave him the ingredients, he mixed them together inside a plastic garbage bag that I had also supplied and kept it in his toilet for a little over a week while it fermented. The bag had to be kept tightly sealed because it emitted an unmistakable odor as it went through the fermentation process. And as it fermented, pressure built that had to be relieved several times a day. I ran interference with the guards, keeping them as far away from Buff's cell as possible while he slowly bled the pressure off the bag.

When it was ready, he signaled that it was time. I'd never tasted hooch before, but I'd imagined it clear and sweet with a fruity aftertaste and a low alcohol content. It turned out to be light brown in color with mashed up grapefruit pulp floating on top; it was absolutely the most foul-tasting, nauseating thing I'd ever tasted, but I still drank it and tried to enjoy it.

Two weeks after my arrival, just as I was getting used to El Reno, hooch, and my orderly duties, I was told I was leaving. The following morning I was on the road again, this time in a US Marshals' van transporting me to Bastrop. *At last*, I thought, *air-conditioning and good food*. I would serve the rest of my time and feel settled.

After we'd been on the road for about four hours, we pulled into a roadside park so we could use the restroom. The five of us were handcuffed with our legs shackled as they herded us through the middle of the park, past a number of picnicking families. We caused a bit of a sensation, especially among the children. I don't know how many kids there were—at least ten or twelve, from toddlers to young teenagers, and they came running at us, trying to get close enough to get a good look. Even funnier were their hysterical parents, especially the mothers, chasing after them and pulling them to safety. When we came out of the restrooms, the kids were still waiting for us, though by then their parents had them corralled at a safe distance. I felt like an animal again, like a lion in a zoo.

My first sight of Bastrop was more than a little surprising. After being locked up in the crumbling prisons of Atlanta and El Reno, it looked like a college campus, at least once I got through the double fences and razor wire. The buildings were new. It was clean and air-conditioned.

Security was high, though. Not long before I arrived, there had been an escape attempt in which several convicts managed to get a .357 magnum smuggled inside and had taken several guards hostage. In the end nobody was seriously hurt, but this incident had resulted in a strict and by-the-book system. The convicts were marched everywhere they went surrounded by guards; controlled movement was strictly enforced. Body searches and shakedowns of our cells were done continuously.

I had my own cell, which didn't have normal bars on the windows but something like metal sheeting with small holes so the light could filter through. I was so relieved to finally be where I was going to stay and no longer in transit, a place I could call home for the next few years. Or so I thought.

I was in the chow hall on my second day when Bill walked in.

"Bill!" I hollered, and when he turned and saw me, he looked as though he'd seen a ghost. He'd had no idea I was coming to Bastrop. We had a fine time catching up while we ate lunch. I think he was as glad to see someone he knew from the outside as I was. We wouldn't be able to see each other too much because we weren't in the same cell block, but at least we could count on meals. I also comforted myself with the fact that mail would soon be trickling in once my family and friends found out my permanent address.

Outside of receiving a visitor, which I hadn't had yet, mail call is the single-most-important part of prison life.

All the rules at Bastrop took some getting used to, but after a week, or so I began to relax. Bastrop seemed like it was going to be an okay place to do time. And then early one morning in my second week, I was awakened and told that I was being transferred. The guard who came to my cell didn't know where I was being transferred or why; he just ordered me to get dressed and be ready to report to R&D in fifteen minutes.

Despite my vow to remain positive no matter what, this news was a cruel shock. And underneath the shock, I was furious and confused. But of course I had nowhere to show my anger and no one to show it to. I had to swallow it, but it was hard. When I arrived at R&D, I was informed that I was being transferred to a prison in Englewood, Colorado. I found out later that a federal lawsuit brought by a prisoner sentenced under the Federal Youth Corrections Act had forced the Bureau of Prisons to house all convicts sentenced under this act in dedicated prisons. Bastrop was not a designated youth offender prison.

Four hours after receiving this news, I was on the Bureau of Prisons airplane, but my destination wasn't Englewood. I was flying back to El Reno, where I'd been less than three weeks before.

Even today, I shake my head at the inefficiencies of the prison system. Why does the Bureau of Prisons transfer convicts around the country for no discernible reason? It cannot be fiscally responsible; it has to cost the taxpayers more money. I'd been incarcerated for about seven months and had been in prisons in New Orleans, Tallahassee, Atlanta, El Reno, and Bastrop, and now I was going back to El Reno and then on to Englewood, Colorado.

It certainly contributes to the dehumanization of the convicts, stripping them of personal control over their lives. This is the lesson you are supposed to learn: don't ask why; don't make trouble; don't think. Just obey. But that's not the lesson I learned. I discovered that it didn't matter what they took away or what they did. If

The Malvaney family, 1959–60: (*left to right, top to bottom*) George's father, Louis; George's mother, Gwen; Lucienne; baby George; Corinne; and Sam.

Three-year-old George, 1962.

Six-year-old George collecting beaver cuttings on a creek adjacent to the Pearl River, 1966.

The USS *Concord* (AFS-5), where George Malvaney organized and led a KKK unit.

George Malvaney (*center front*) and the other nine mercenaries involved with the Bayou of Pigs plot entering the Orleans Parish Prison, April 1981. AP Photo/Jack Thornell.

The US Penitentiary in Atlanta.

George Malvaney (*kneeling, left*) with other convicts, Federal Correctional Institute, Englewood, Colorado, 1982. Photo by Jaycees photographer.

Convict friends of George Malvaney at the Federal Correctional Institute, Englewood, Colorado, 1982. Five of the seven convicts shown are American Indians. Photo by Jaycees photographer.

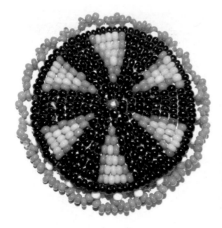

The pendant that George Malvaney received from Old Man Paddy while at the Federal Correctional Institute, Englewood, Colorado.

L. E. Matthews sitting at a table behind his house, 1984. This is the same table where George removed the serial numbers from sticks of dynamite and first met Byron De La Beckwith.

George Malvaney (*left*) and Dr. Kenny Williams (*far right*), with rebel flag displayed in support of Ole Miss. Alligator Bayou Hunting Camp, Wilkinson County, Mississippi, 1984–85.

Louis and Gwen Malvaney at church,
St. Patrick's Day, ca. 1985–90.

George and Louis Malvaney at
George's wedding, 1989.

Forrest and Hillary Malvaney, Hopewell, Mississippi, 1994.

George Malvaney (*center front*), Mississippi governor Haley Barbour (*right*), and BP's Kenny Spriggs exiting a Blackhawk helicopter after a tour of the BP oil slick off the Mississippi Gulf Coast, May 2010.

George Malvaney talking with US Representative Gene Taylor after touring a BP staging area, June 2010. Courtesy of the *Sun Herald*.

George Malvaney (*standing*) briefing Governor Barbour and his staff on defensive measures to prevent the BP oil slick from reaching the Mississippi Gulf Coast, May 2010. Photo by Dan M. Turner.

Forrest Malvaney (*center front*) handling oil protection boom at a BP staging area, Bayou Caddy, Mississippi, 2010. Courtesy of the *Sun Herald*.

Hillary Malvaney and her son, Patrick, 2016.

George Malvaney's writing setup in Montana's Beartooth Mountains, 2015.

I stayed determined and mentally focused, I still had control over my thoughts and emotions. I didn't have to let go of human connections. I didn't have to let them make me feel defeated or despondent. I could remain upbeat and positive and take what I could from this experience. I could become a better person if I wanted to. So I did.

CHAPTER TEN

Keeping the Peace

After a couple of days in El Reno, I was put on another Bureau of Prisons plane en route to Stapleton Airport in Denver. A prison bus met about thirty of us at the airport to drive us to our newest destination, Englewood Federal Correctional Institute in Littleton, Colorado.

The ride was uneventful, but one thing does stand out: at some point along our trip, our bus passed two very nice looking female hitchhikers. Even though the weather was cool, one of them was wearing short shorts and a halter top. It doesn't take much imagination to know what response this got from a bunch of sexually deprived convicts in our late teens and early twenties. I don't think the girls could hear the hooting, but they could certainly see a lot of faces leering at them from between the bars on the windows. I wasn't catcalling—that wasn't my style—but I admit that I stared, too. It had been a long time since I'd had any female company or even seen a female other than a prison guard or staffer.

I hoped this was an omen of better things to come.

Englewood had a reputation as a laid-back joint, an okay place to do time. A large number of the cons there had been transferred from McNeil Island Penitentiary in Washington State when it closed, and most of them were older and just wanted to do their bit and get by with as little trouble as possible. Many other cons at Englewood were Native Americans—mostly Sioux, Crow, and

Apache from New Mexico, Colorado, Montana, and the Dakotas. They were a close-knit group and tended to keep to themselves.

Englewood wasn't always laid back. The Native Americans in particular were a tough bunch. Almost all were in for murder—murder on a reservation is a federal offense, so they were incarcerated at a federal prison. My group of newcomers found out how tough the Native Americans were by the second day.

On the ride to Englewood, a group of about ten East Coast blacks had formed a clique and openly boasted about how they were going to run the new joint. These men made the mistake of jumping on one of the "chiefs," as the Native Americans were called, out in the prison yard. No group is more protective of each other, and within fifteen minutes those young toughs were running for their lives with a war party of Indians after them. Some of them were so scared that they "checked in" to solitary confinement, where it was safer. The remainder of the gang was like a den of whipped pups, cowering in the open dorm of our unit. That evening, there was talk going around among the chiefs about "riding on the niggers." The tension was thick for a while, but it died down—the chiefs decided they just weren't worth it.

I didn't dwell on being transferred out of Bastrop and sent to Colorado. There wasn't anything I could do about it. I hoped that they wouldn't transfer me again, but I didn't think about that possibility either. Instead I concentrated on laying low.

Englewood had four separate units for housing convicts. Each had an open dorm and two ranges of one-man cells. I was assigned to Upper East cell block. Unless you broke the rules and were sent to the Hole, there was some semblance of freedom. And we had jobs—menial jobs, of course, but as I'd learned in El Reno, any job is better than doing nothing.

My first assignment was as a janitor in the Vo-Tech Center. Mostly I pushed around a mop and broom. One of the instructors was a Jewish man who took an interest in me. Although I was a year or so removed from being an active Klansman and he was very liberal, we struck up a friendship. He encouraged me to pursue an education after I was paroled. He also told me that I needed to learn how to type if I was going to attend college, so I enrolled in the prison typing class that he taught. We used electric typewriters—computers and word processors had not yet become common—and before long I was typing 110 words per minute.

After I got to know the guards in Upper East pretty well, I angled for a job in the unit laundry, and they gave it to me. I wanted to work in the laundry because it was totally unsupervised and meant that I had more freedom.

Although I didn't know anyone when I arrived at Englewood, I started to make friends, guys I could talk to and hang out with. Tom was in for bank robbery, a smart and easygoing guy who went on to become a physician. Don, a Native American from Denver who was in for some violent crime that I can't recall, was a potentially dangerous guy, but I liked him. He stuck up for his beliefs. Ramon and Rogelio were Hispanic drug dealers with whom I became close friends. Kevin, a bank robber from Washington State, was a stand-up con. There were a host of Native Americans—Red Fox, Shooter, Bear Quiver, and Wooden Thigh—all of them in for murder. My closest friend was Jerry Wood, known as the Wood, a burly biker who had committed a laundry list of federal crimes. I began developing black friends, too. I came to like Snow, who was also housed in Upper East. Snow was a stand-up con and respected by all. Greg, a bank robber from California, had a strong racist streak and didn't really like whites, but we got along well and eventually reached the point where we could discuss racial issues.

I acquired a nickname. My friend Wood gave it to me. There weren't many southerners at Englewood, and my thick Mississippi accent made me stand out. Wood said I sounded like the cartoon character Huckleberry Hound, so he started calling me Huckleberry. Pretty soon most everyone was calling me that, and then it was shortened to Huck.

In prison there's a ranking system based on your crime—child molesters and child killers are the lowest of the low, even lower than rapists. In federal prison we didn't get many of these, because those are predominantly state crimes. But my crime earned me some respect.

We did receive a child killer at Englewood shortly after my arrival, however. Quinn Amaro arrived from California, where he had murdered four members of an entire family and stolen their guns. The murders were committed on federal property, so they became federal crimes. One of the people he killed was a two-year-old toddler; another young girl was shot five times. Quinn was assigned to Upper East, and his cell was across from mine and maybe six or eight down.

One night, I was awakened by a commotion coming from down the cell block. A little while later, I heard a helicopter land in the prison yard. It was a medevac helicopter coming to transport Quinn to a Denver emergency room. He had been attacked by a group of stand-up convicts in retribution for being a child killer. They'd bashed his skull in with a blunt object and stabbed him multiple times in the chest with a shank. Despite the ferocity and viciousness of the attack, Quinn survived. The cons that rolled in on him caught new cases and received more time, but they did what they had to do. One of these cons, Red, was a friend of mine. I respected him more after what he'd done.

Racism is a fact of life in prison. Everything inside is racially charged, and you have to accept it. Racial slurs were like vanilla ice cream—they didn't stand out because they were so common. Lines are drawn, and you have to learn fast which side you're on. The racial line is obvious, but there are others as well—between convicts and guards, between the statuses associated with different types of crimes. Prison is a microcosm of the worst of society, and the lines help prevent chaos.

I tried to get along with all of the various groups—the chiefs, the Hispanics, the blacks, the whites. I had discussions with people who had views and histories that were radically different than mine, but my conversations were motivated out of interest more than animosity. I developed a reputation as a person who could get along with everyone, and as a result, I was chosen as the white representative to the Inmate Advisory Committee. The committee had one black con, one white, one Native American, and one Hispanic. Prison administrators chose the representatives, seeking out guys who were respected by their own race as well as others because sometimes we were called on to help defuse racial issues. I found it ironic that I was the only ex-Klansman in the prison and yet they chose me as the white guy who could get along well with other racial groups.

The Hispanic convicts had a prison association that was part of a national civil rights group, La Raza. On a number of occasions, the Denver chapter came to the prison and put on an event exclusively for the Hispanic convicts. I got invited to all of their functions and I was always the only non-Hispanic there.

One large La Raza event that was held in the prison cafeteria. Quite a few Hispanics from the streets (prison slang for the outside world) were there when I arrived with Ramon as his guest. I was the only non-Hispanic in attendance (all of the guards were Hispanic), and most everyone was speaking in Spanish. When I first arrived, I got a few stares until a few of the prisoners explained that I was a friend. I couldn't understand much of what was being said, but I didn't let that stop me from mixing with the crowd. I joined in on the festivities and had a great time. When it was over and I was leaving, one of the Hispanic guards looked at me and laughingly said, "This is the first time I've ever seen a gringo at a La Raza event. And not just any gringo—a Mississippi Klansman, at that."

The white convicts were represented by an outside civic group, the Jaycees. I was designated as the state director of the Englewood unit, but it was a rather lame group and I never got heavily involved. I still have my Jaycees pin with *State Director* printed on it.

I also got along well with the Native Americans and actually made quite a few good friends among them even though they were the most racially closed group. The Native Americans really only associated with each other, perhaps because they're part of a tribal culture. Apaches were the most closed and potentially violent tribe. But whichever tribe, if you got into an altercation with one Native American, you had to fight every one of them. And they could be violent—they all had access to shanks and weren't afraid to use them. For some reason, though, they genuinely liked me and, more important, trusted me.

Upper East had an older Native American, Paddy, who had been in prison for many years and by that time was probably in his midseventies. He was serving a life sentence for murder. Old Man Paddy mostly kept to himself, but I became close with him. He was soft-spoken, but his face told the story of a hard life: his features were chiseled, and he had deep lines crisscrossing his face, which reminded me of a road map. His complexion was dark, and his gray hair was always neatly slicked back.

Sometimes he'd drop by the laundry room to talk with me. If the washers and dryers weren't running, I could hear his feet slowly shuffling across the concrete floor as he approached the door.

"Old Man Paddy—don't be sneaking up on me like an Indian brave," I'd holler.

He always chuckled and would just stand there smiling. We shared a love of the outdoors and could talk about hunting and fishing for hours.

He was eventually transferred out of Englewood as it continued to evolve into a prison dedicated to those sentenced under the Federal Youth Corrections Act. The afternoon before he was to be transferred, he came by the laundry room with a gift for me. It was a pendant about the size of a silver dollar. It had a leather back with a safety pin clasp, and the front was decorated with small beads.

He thrust it into the palm of my right hand and covered my fist with his other hand. "I made this for you," he said. "Thank you for being my friend." Then he turned and shuffled out of the laundry room. It was an emotional moment for both of us.

That night as I lay on the bunk, I examined the pendant. The beads were red, orange, and black with a single silver bead in the center. They were tiny, about four hundred of them total, the best I could count. I lay there wondering just how long Old Man Paddy had endeavored to make this gift for me with his arthritic hands. I still have it today, and I treasure it as much as anything I own.

At the opposite end of the spectrum was a young Sioux, Red Fox. Much like Old Man Paddy, he was quiet and tended to be a loner. Red Fox was in his early twenties and had long jet-black hair; he wore a red bandana around his head. He was very difficult to get to know because he didn't speak much to anyone, especially anyone who wasn't a Native American. But we developed a friendship despite these things and had conversations on a regular basis.

During a routine shakedown, Red Fox was busted with a shank in his cell and was written up and sent to the Hole. A few days after he was locked down in solitary, a guard approached me and said that Red Fox wanted me to attend his disciplinary hearing to speak on his behalf. This was a very unusual request, but I readily agreed.

We went before one of the deputy wardens and a few other prison staffers; I knew everyone in the hearing and got along well with all of them. I told the deputy warden that Red Fox was an exemplary convict. "He hasn't been in any trouble prior to this and is known as a quiet individual who never causes problems," I said. All of it was true.

I knew it was futile to argue that the shank wasn't his, however, so I had to come up with some kind of argument on his behalf. "The prison administration is partially to blame for Red Fox having a shank in his cell," I said. "If y'all were doing your jobs, he wouldn't feel the need to have a weapon to defend himself from attack."

The deputy warden's lips formed a thin smile as I continue to blame them for Red Fox having a shank in his possession. This was a first. They were accustomed to convicts denying that the shank was theirs, claiming it was a setup. After I finished my argument, the deputy warden asked Red Fox if it was indeed his shank. Red Fox quietly replied that it was. And then the disciplinary committee had a brief discussion while we sat there. After a while, the warden said with some amusement, "Nice try, Malvaney, but your argument doesn't pass muster." Red Fox would spend ten days in isolation. He sat completely emotionless and didn't say a word. He had gotten off lightly for a major infraction, and he knew it.

I'd acquired a TV in my cell, which added to my popularity among many of the convicts in Upper East. That was against the rules, of course, but it had been smuggled in to my Hispanic drug dealer friend, Ramon. He'd probably paid a lot of money for it as well as a lot of money to pay off the guards so that he could to keep it.

When Ramon was transferred to another prison, he gave it to me because I was his friend and because I was the only convict at Englewood who might be able to keep it without having it confiscated. Sometimes in the late afternoons after work was over, whites, Native Americans, and Hispanics would hang out in my cell and we'd watch TV together. Sports events were always popular, especially boxing. They'd also talk freely about their lives. Sometimes the chiefs talked about putting hits on the black cons, and they trusted me not to say anything to the guards about the plans or the shanks.

I even got along well with the guards. Several of them genuinely liked and respected me and therefore allowed me special privileges. When they made their regular shakedowns throughout the cells looking for contraband, they ignored the TV. They'd look right at it and walk on by as if it wasn't there. They didn't even ask for anything in return, which was fortunate because I had nothing to bribe them with. I used to have friendly discussions with some of the guards, too, and got to know a few of them on a more personal level. I didn't have anything against them; they were just doing their jobs, and their jobs were not easy.

Ramon had also gotten an electric hot plate smuggled in, and we kept it in the Upper East laundry room where only the guards and I could go. Every once in a while, we'd get some guards to smuggle in beef, chicken, onions, and bell peppers, and Ramon, Rogelio, and a couple of the other Hispanic cons would gather in the laundry room where we cooked and made burritos. Sometimes we invited one of the night guards to eat with us. One night I invited a hard-nosed white guy we called Gunslinger. He was a tall, lanky cowboy and was generally a strict disciplinarian. I got along well with Gunslinger; we often talked about hunting.

"Huck, how in the hell do you get along so well with Rogelio and the other racist Mexicans?" he asked.

"I just do," I said. "Now come eat."

After I'd been at Englewood for a few months, my parents flew out from Mississippi for a visit. In the visitors' room, I noticed that my dad had on a pair of new cowboy boots, really nice ones. Of course we weren't allowed to wear boots— only the standard prison-issued shoes. But I looked at my dad's boots and I wanted them—they looked like freedom and Mississippi rolled into one.

"Good-looking boots," I said. Dad smiled and offered to send me a pair just like them. "That won't work. They'd never get past the mailroom." I paused for a moment and said, "But we might be able to trade."

So we did. We waited for a time when the guard was looking else-where, and Dad took off his boots and I removed my prison shoes. Then we quietly slipped our feet into our new footwear.

I knew I'd be strip-searched before they took me back to my cell block, and I was hoping the guard would be one of the friendly ones who let me get away with things. I was lucky. The guard was a Hispanic guy named Guyegas with whom I'd had some fine conversations. He just smiled and shook his head as he motioned me inside. I heard later that the prison shoes had set off the security alarm and they'd made my father take them off to be searched. That made me laugh and appreciate those cowboy boots even more.

I also became friends with a prison caseworker named Zamparelli. Like me, Zamp loved guns and was a proponent of the Second Amendment. He was a member of the NRA and used to bring the organization's magazine in to me. (The prison frowned upon gun literature for convicts. I guess they thought it would make us more violent.)

At that time, the early 1980s, a lot of noise was being made about passing laws on gun control. An Illinois town banned handguns, and Zamp and I spent time discussing that law and reading about it in the papers. Advocates of gun control claimed it would cut the violent crime rate, and it gave me an idea. What better place to conduct a poll on gun control than in a prison with violent crime offenders? Would laws stop them from obtaining or using a gun?

I made a questionnaire with issues from both supporters and opponents of gun control as well as some of my own. Over a three-week period in the spring of 1982, I questioned fifty convicts from all four of the main racial groups. The results were clear: they overwhelmingly thought that gun control was unworkable, useless, and stupid. As one hard-core convict told me, "As long as police have guns, I will carry a gun, and I'll be able to get one. No matter what laws they pass." He was saying that he was willing to kill a police officer to get a gun if necessary.

I showed the poll and the results to Zamp, and he suggested I write it up as an article and send it to the NRA magazine. To my surprise, my article appeared in the group's May newsletter. It was also published in July in a newsletter put out by the Citizens Committee for the Right to Keep and Bear Arms. Zamp brought me some copies, and I showed them around. I think the guys in prison were proud that their views had been taken seriously by those on the street. I, too, was proud of this project and its results. It was a positive thing, and I was always looking for ways to stay positive.

If you let it, prison can be an effective school; it's the ultimate University of Hard Knocks. It changes you, no matter what, but each person chooses which changes to keep. Most convicts let their anger and ignorance grow in response to their prison experiences, the majority of which are negative. After all, you're surrounded by the worst that society has to offer. Convicts often let themselves be driven by these negative and violent emotions. I tried to do it another way and lead with my rational brain. I don't deny that I had negative thoughts, but I didn't let them consume me. I focused on what I was going to do and be in the future. What I'd done and thought in the past had clearly not worked, so I tried to look at what I wanted to change about myself, and figure out how to bring about those changes.

When I first went to prison, I was extremely racist. I thought blacks were low-life scum, but after my letter-writing experiences with Leon in Atlanta as well as others, I questioned my beliefs. My outlook continued to evolve in Englewood, as I met a lot of people from very different backgrounds. I had discussions with black convicts from the West Coast, Native Americans from New Mexico to the Dakotas, and Hispanics from the Southwest, and we worked at getting along. We didn't always stay agreeable, but we tried.

Deep-seated racist beliefs do not go away overnight, no matter how intellectual you are. Sometimes I still viewed the black convicts as lowlifes, but other times I could see that they were people like me, only with different experiences. The bottom line was that I had begun to understand that I could *choose* what to believe.

Another change was my outlook toward authority and the government. Prior to my arrest, I was extremely right wing: a supporter of individual rights and a strong military and anticommunist. One reason the Klan had appealed to me was because it proclaimed our right to oppose, violently if necessary, laws we did not agree with or that infringed on our freedom. While in prison, it became obvious to me that this militant noncompromising attitude did not work. Antagonizing people is rarely the best way to get your point across. I learned that nearly all people, even those who'd done terrible things, wanted their families to be fed and happy, and no one set out to be wrong or bad. There were ways to get along with everyone, no matter what their race or politics.

One thing that didn't change was my attitude toward the law. I was never opposed to authority, but I was opposed to excessive authority. Prison solidified this outlook. The way that prisons are run is not only stupid but criminal. They're nothing more than factories that churn out bitter, dangerous ex-cons who go on to commit crimes of even greater violence. People convicted of nonviolent or relatively minor felonies are thrown in with dangerous and cruel monsters and then often become monsters because they believe it's the only way to survive.

I considered getting a law degree. I knew for sure I needed to get an education. I wasn't certain what I wanted to do—maybe it would be law, maybe not. Engineering (like my father), biology, or wildlife management all sounded good to me, too, especially since I could be outdoors. If I wanted to achieve any of the lofty goals I'd set or break the patterns of the past, I had to be educated.

When I got out, I was determined that I would get a college degree—I would be a good student and make good grades. I was also beginning to realize just how much my life and goals had changed in less than five years. I'd gone from being a bottom-of-the-barrel student and high school dropout in 1977 to a dedicated Klansman to a convict making black friends while planning to enroll in college. And every single day, I thought back on my "Cups up" moment and the commitment I'd made to myself in Tallahassee. It seemed like eons ago. So much had changed.

I also realized that when I got out, I would have to start hanging around people who were not prone to criminal activities. So many people in prison were uneducated dropouts with no plans for what to do when they were released. They were just going to go back to doing what they'd always done. My chief friend, Don, said the first thing he wanted to do was get his hands on a pump shotgun. He daydreamed about going down to the river to practice shooting all damn day, and said he still had his AR-15 and an M-1 hidden somewhere. He was going to get magazines for them and then attend the first Soldier of Fortune convention he could find. That was his whole plan. I could see that when he did get released, he would soon be back.

If I didn't want to do the same, I had to correct the path I'd been following, which meant I had to change the people I'd been hanging out with. I'd had enough of living with criminals who had done terrible things and whose lifestyles and patterns were keeping them stuck. If I associated with people who tended to get involved in illegal activities, there was a likelihood I'd end up back in prison. I didn't want to completely disown people I liked, like Dannie Hawkins, but I wanted to distance myself from them and their beliefs.

I was going to make myself a better person. Period.

I'd been at Englewood less than a year when I was called before the parole board. I knew that those sentenced under the Youth Correction Act typically had to serve most or all of their time, so I wasn't expecting to be paroled, and the board members acted exactly as I figured they would, recommending that I serve my four years. After learning of their actions, however, my sentencing judge, Lansing Mitchell from New Orleans, intervened to get me an early release date. My sentence was reduced to eighteen months, which I was rapidly approaching.

It was a great feeling—totally exhilarating.

My cell on the second floor had a small barred window where I could see a large grassy field and a housing development far in the distance. I spent countless hours looking out that window, gazing at those tiny people going in and out of their houses and cars, living their normal lives, doing whatever they wanted or needed to do. I so wanted to be one of them, free to take care of my own concerns. *Free.* The most beautiful word there is.

After receiving my parole date, I spent more hours gazing out that window. I thought about what I'd do when I was released: go fishing, frog-gigging, and hunting. I badly wanted female companionship. *I'm never coming back here*, I thought. It's the thought that went through my head the most.

My last night in prison was rather uneventful. A group of cons gathered in my cell that evening—a select group of whites, Native Americans, and Hispanics. We smoked marijuana and reminisced about all of the good times we'd shared. (I had never used drugs or smoked marijuana prior to my incarceration, but I did come to partake in a joint now and then to help ease the pain of imprisonment.)

The morning of my release, I went by Wood's cell. His last words were, "I hate to see you go, Huck." It was a powerful moment, and in a strange sort of way, I hated to be leaving my prison buds. And then I walked out of Upper East to the Administration Building and on to freedom.

It was an unbelievable feeling when I walked out the entrance of Englewood. "Cups up, cups up," I said.

Now, thirty-something years later, I'm able to see that prison was the most important learning experience of my life. If I could go back in time and plead not guilty and get off like Mike Norris did, I wouldn't do it. Prison was a wonderfully terrible experience, a dichotomy of the most extreme sorts. It awakened a deep soul-searching that was often painful and set into motion a process of change that might otherwise never have occurred. I saw brutal attacks, heads beaten in, viciousness of all kinds. I lived with people who'd committed horrible crimes, and some of those people became my friends. It's all a part of me now.

PART THREE

George would be so livid, so furious, when he found people burying poisons and then trying to cover up what they did, but at the same time he was happy that he had this big regulatory stick and could make them take responsibility and clean up their mess. And when George said clean, he meant clean.

—**Gloria Tatum,** Mississippi Department of Environmental Quality

CHAPTER ELEVEN

1982–Present: Evolution Takes Time

During my flight home, reality set in. I was free, but my thoughts quickly shifted to what I was going to do now. I reflected on that first morning in Tallahassee and was determined to hold myself accountable.

When I got off the plane in Jackson, my sister, Lucienne, and a few friends met me at the gate. My father was working in Nevada at the time, so my parents couldn't make it. It was emotional, of course. What else could it be?

I was home.

I was going to follow through with my plan to get an education, but college wasn't cheap, and I knew it was my responsibility to pay my own way. Thankfully, Lucienne agreed to let me live with her so I'd be able to save enough money to enroll in the spring of 1983.

I went to visit my grandmother, Nana, the afternoon of my first day out of prison. She was still the fireball that she'd always been. Nana gave me a big hug and then proceeded to really chew my ass out about getting involved in such a crazy scheme. I promised her that I was going to turn my life around and make her proud of me, and I meant it.

On my first full day of freedom, I went to see my old boss, Ricky Turner, who hired me on the spot. He was still doing residential construction and remodeling and had also bought a Jackson business, the Beer Barn Drive Thru. It was exactly what the name implied—a barn-shaped building that you drove into and ordered beer without having to get out of your car. I didn't have a vehicle or any means of transportation, so Ricky was kind enough to pick me up every morning. I worked all day doing construction and then nights and weekends at the Beer Barn. In what little spare time I had, I went into the woods and swamps, sometimes to fish and sometimes to do not much of anything, just getting used to freedom again. All those hours watching the outside through bars and wondering how it would feel when I got out—now I knew. I could go wherever I wanted, when I wanted. I could go to the swamp or the store, or I could simply walk around my sister's yard. I didn't have to ask anyone for permission. I wasn't watched. I could feel the wind on my skin, the skin that belonged to me again.

My prison experience sometimes proved useful, though, like the night there was a robbery at the Beer Barn. My co-worker, Lee Speed, and I were closing when she went out to her car to find that it had been broken into and her purse stolen. She came back in and called the police. The Beer Barn had garage-type doors on either end, and we had pulled them down but not locked them since we were waiting for the police to arrive. Suddenly, one of the doors flew open and two young thugs ran inside. One of the guys had a revolver.

They were real professionals. The one with the revolver never got within eight or ten feet of us and kept the gun trained at my head. I looked directly into his eyes, which were cold and expressionless. These guys meant business, and I sensed that they wouldn't hesitate to kill us if we resisted or didn't comply with their demands, so I told Lee to do exactly as they said.

The guy without the gun ordered us to lie facedown on the concrete drive while he searched us. He took my wallet and a cheap Timex watch before turning to Lee.

"Gimme your ring," he said.

Her ring was a family heirloom diamond, and she had a strong sentimental attachment to it, so she instinctively clinched her fist. I noticed it instantly and told her as calmly as possible to give him the ring. She wiggled it off her finger. Then they ordered us into the small office where the safe was. The guy with the gun stopped outside of the door and kept the gun trained on my head. I had opened the safe and removed the cash a few minutes before the robbers arrived, and the money—about two thousand dollars—was spread across the desktop where I'd just counted it. The guy ordered us onto the floor and began scooping cash into a bag.

"Hey bud, you're dropping it," I said in a calm and friendly voice as I picked up several bills and handed them to him.

"Thanks, man," he said. I noticed a distinct change in his voice, a softening, so I jokingly told him that I would load them down with all the beer they could ever drink if they wanted me to. He halfway smiled at my joke.

I was trying to be as relaxed as possible in an attempt to keep them calm. Make no mistake—I was scared. I knew all too well what kind of thugs I was dealing with. They were capable of killing us both. I couldn't show any fear or weakness, but I also had to be cooperative and nonthreatening. For the past couple years I'd been dealing with criminals a whole lot meaner and tougher than these young thugs, and I knew that they were a hell of a lot more nervous than I was: that made them dangerous. I was mostly concerned that the police would arrive and people might get hurt. I figured the faster they got the money, the faster they would leave.

They did, and we got off the floor. As soon as they left, Lee started crying, but she had been a real trouper throughout the robbery. The police arrived just a few minutes later. The whole episode reinforced what I'd learned in prison about dealing with violent criminals: keep your cool, don't show any weakness, and with a little bit of luck, you might come out of a bad situation with your life.

They never caught the robbers, and in a way I was glad. I had decided that I couldn't testify against them if they were caught. Convicts don't roll like that. Although I was an ex-con, I still thought like a convict.

The experience at the Beer Barn highlighted another change I wanted to make: criminals were not the kind of people I wanted in my life. But my past associations with the Klan meant that many of my social contacts were just those sorts of people. Slowly at first, I began to pull away from them—easier said than done, of course. I'm a loyal person. I don't discard my friends simply because I don't like their opinions or actions. I also maintained contact with a number of the friends I'd made in prison. We had become close, I suspect because prison is sort of like war—you develop bonds with people who have had the same intense, shared experiences. While I knew it was probably best to let those friendships drift away, it was difficult.

I made a conscious effort to spend more time with my friends from high school. I contacted some of my old buddies, guys who enjoyed hunting and fishing like I did. Some of them had gone on to college, while others had gone straight to work.

I particularly enjoyed going the deer camp that belonged to my friend Ken Williams's father, Kenny, a Jackson radiologist. The camp, Alligator Bayou, was on the Homochitto River swamps near Lake Mary in Wilkinson County, Mississippi. Alligator Bayou was a paradise to me—almost thirteen hundred acres of bottomland hardwood forests, swamps, creeks, and lakes. The deer hunting was phenomenal but there was so much more to do than hunt deer. Although I was still a convicted felon, I felt safe carrying a gun because we were deep in the swamps and access was very difficult.

Ken often invited me and a few other friends to spend time there. Steve Tidwell and I were regulars at Alligator Bayou. We rode three-wheelers, hunted beavers and coons at night, blew up beaver dams with dynamite, fished in the Homochitto, and even caught baby alligators on occasion. There was always plenty of whiskey and fried deer meat. We slept in the camp house, a crude three-room structure consisting of a bunkroom, a kitchen, and a bathroom. The camp house was cold in the winter and hot in the summer.

Other regulars at Alligator Bayou included several of Dr. Williams's close friends or relatives. A real cast of characters they were: Benny, Earl, Dr. Turner, A. G., and Dr. Wennerlund. At night we had a roaring fire in front of the camp house, and the conversation always turned to politics after a certain point. They could best be described as staunchly right-wing. Dr. Wennerlund, a prominent Jackson dentist, often described Alligator Bayou as "not exactly a hotbed of liberal thought."

Dr. Williams liked to cook chitterlings (pig guts), and sometimes we played pranks on visitors. We'd add chopped corn to the batter before frying the chitterlings. When one of the visitors would bite down on a piece of corn, it would be too hard to chew, and they would have to spit it out. Then Dr. Williams would tell them that we never cleaned all the crap out of the guts because that's where they got their flavor. The visitors always had the same reactions: no more pig guts for them, thanks. I had many special times at Alligator Bayou, and those experiences helped me move away from my old prison and Klan associates and get back to my friends from childhood.

I was still receiving letters from my prison pals Don and Wood, who had been transferred to higher-security prisons following a race riot at Englewood shortly after I was released. The riot was primarily between the black and white convicts, but several of the chiefs were involved, fighting side by side with the whites. One of the Indians involved was Don, who was transferred to a prison in Petersburg, Virginia. A few months later, I received a letter from him: "Hey bro, hope all is fine for you. As for me, here in Little Africa it is really fucked up, where there are enough niggers to start a Tarzan movie. I got sent here with a plane load of rioters. Controlled movement all week long, nothing to do here but work out. The food sucks and there are nothing but toads everywhere. Pussy and guns are the good life, if only I could convince the courts that."

According to Don, tear gas raids and stabbings were common. He asked me to help him get him some guns when he was released. My best prison bud, Wood, was also transferred to Petersburg and wrote to me about the violence in "boot lip city" and how he'd seen a hack get killed in a brawl. When I read the letters, I mostly felt sorry for them. They hadn't changed, but I had.

Though I maintained contact with several of my prison buds during this time, the only ones I ever saw in person after I was paroled were Tom and Wood. Tom was the laidback bank robber. He was released earlier than I was; in fact, he was released the same day that my parents had come to visit, so they got to meet him and even drove him to the bus station. Tom was from Wisconsin and was impressed by southern friendliness—how my parents had gone out of their way to help him. When he heard I was released, he rode his motorcycle all the way to Mississippi for a visit. He had a great time, especially learning how to eat crawfish while enjoying ice-cold beer. Like me, Tom had reached a turning point in prison, and after enjoying a few years of freedom, he enrolled in college and then medical school, and now he's a physician.

I saw Wood a couple of years after my release when he was paroled and living in Texas. I visited him one weekend, and it was great to see him on the streets. I saw him again a few years later when I was a college student living in Hattiesburg, Mississippi. He came to visit, and we had a grand time reminiscing and catching up. Wood was a hell of a guy, a stand-up convict and a great friend who would have done almost anything for me. But in my heart, I knew that I had to break ties with my old prison buds who still had criminal tendencies. His trip to Hattiesburg was the last time I ever saw him.

Eventually I cut all ties with everyone except Dr. Tom. He and I are friends to this day and still see one another on occasion.

More difficult to disengage with were Dannie Hawkins, L. E. Matthews, and Sam Bowers. They were not stereotypical Klansmen and weren't ignorant men; they encouraged me to get an education and make something of my life. I came to know Bowers well, and he always encouraged me to stick with my studies and obtain my degree. When I was looking at colleges shortly after I was paroled, I visited the University of Southern Mississippi, and I called Sam and told him I was going to be in Hattiesburg. He invited me to spend the night at his house in nearby Laurel.

After my campus visit, I made the short drive to Sam's one late afternoon. He lived in an almost all-black neighborhood in an old commercial building that he'd converted into his home. The inside of his house consisted of a large den, a bathroom, and his bedroom. The front door entered directly into the den with a couch (where I slept) immediately on the right and a bathroom to the far left side. Sam's bedroom was across from the bathroom. The area between the couch and the bathroom was completely full of stack after stack of old newspapers and books and boxes upon boxes of legal documents from his extensive run-ins with the law during his Kluxing days. The room had a slight musty odor.

We sat on his couch and discussed different universities, junior colleges, and possible degrees. Then we went to dinner at a nearby restaurant, Nick's, and continued to talk about my educational goals. "Stick with it no matter what," he said. "An education is an invaluable asset that no one can ever take away from you."

When I left his house the following morning, I knew that I was going to get a college degree. Ironically, I also knew that I needed to start distancing myself from him.

I saw Sam every once in a while but didn't put much energy into the relationship after that. I still liked him and found him interesting to talk to, and I had a memorable conversation with him in 1983 at a Jackson restaurant, Piccadilly. He was really on a roll. Sam liked to talk philosophically about the history and meaning of just about everything, and that day, he spoke about the "natural order of the world" and other subjects such as terrorism and the warlike history of the Catholic Church. When we finally got up to leave after a couple of hours, an older couple who'd been sitting at the table next to us leaned over and apologetically told him that they'd been listening to our conversation the whole time. They were absolutely fascinated and expressed just how much they had enjoyed it. Sam had that effect on people.

Dannie Hawkins had been convicted in 1981 for his part in the Dominica plot but had been out on appeal for several years. He, too, encouraged me to go to college but was less adamant than Sam was. Dannie finally went to prison for his involvement, and I received letters from him after I got out. I saw him every once in a while after he was released, but the times in between got longer and longer and our relationship gradually faded away because I did not pursue it.

L. E. Matthews had been acquitted of all charges associated with financing the Dominica plot. I spent a good bit of time with him and worked odd jobs for him on and off for a couple years after my release.

One of those jobs involved helping L. E. move a cabin he owned from the banks of the Strong River near D'Lo, Mississippi, to his land near Florence. He had leased the Strong River property for many years, but after the land changed hands, the new owners wanted him gone. They sent him a certified letter saying he could relocate his cabin but forbid him from cutting any trees to remove it. They were hoping that he would be forced to leave the cabin so they could use it. Obviously, they didn't know L. E.

Several big oaks seemingly blocked any possibility of moving the cabin, but L. E. was both determined and creative. He tasked me with digging three holes four or five feet down into the roots under the trees. We then placed dynamite into the holes and blasted the trees out of the ground. Once the trees were out of the way, an Amish house mover came in, loaded the cabin onto a trailer, and transported it to L. E's property. We never cut a single tree, just as the landowner had asked.

Several weeks after helping L. E. with this task, I was at his house late one Sunday afternoon. I'd been helping him plant watermelon seedlings, and we were taking a break. As we sat outside at a patio table, an older-model Cadillac pulled up.

"Well, I'll be. It's De La," he muttered in an amused tone.

This was my first introduction to Byron De La Beckwith, one of the most notorious and violent Klansmen of all time. De La was a legendary character. He had twice been tried for the 1963 murder of civil rights leader Medgar Evers, but both trials had resulted in hung juries. Now, here I was, sipping a glass of ice water at the same table where I had removed the serial numbers from dynamite a few years earlier and out of a Cadillac pops De La wearing a crumpled, dark suit.

"De La Beckwith," he said loudly as he extended his hand. We spent the next two hours talking. Or more accurately, he spent the next two hours talking while L. E. and I sat there and listened. I found him to be a very gregarious and outspoken man. It didn't take me long to determine that he was still an avowed and unapologetic racist. Unlike Bowers, who never used the word *nigger*, De La laced it into his conversation frequently.

He removed his suit coat, exposing a double shoulder holster containing two Model 1911 Colt .45 handguns. He laughingly told a story of a recent church service he had attended. "Every time I sat back down after standing for a hymnal you could hear a dual thump from the pistols bumping against the back of the wooden pew. Once this had happened a couple times the lady next to me glanced over to see what was making the sound, and I pulled my coat back so she could see," he said with great amusement.

Over the next year or two, I saw De La maybe three or four times. Each time it was at L. E.'s house, and each time he was the same old De La. I never got to know him nearly as well as I did Dannie, L. E., and Sam, but I knew him well enough to know that he was a racist through and through.

It wasn't long after meeting him that I moved to Hattiesburg and began drifting further and further away from L. E. He died in 1993, and I attended his funeral. I hadn't seen him in a long while and found myself regretting not having visited him during his long period of sickness. His funeral was small and attended by a diverse crowd of cronies from his Kluxing days. Sam Bowers and Dannie Hawkins were there—Bowers was a pallbearer—along with a few lesser-known Klan figures.

But the preacher was Rev. Ken Dean, who served as director of the Mississippi Council of Human Relations, a civil rights group, in the 1960s and 1970s and who had forged relationships with L. E., Hawkins, and Bowers. Also in attendance was Bill Minor of the *Jackson Clarion-Ledger*. L. E. and Bill had known each other since way back when Bill was a reporter with the *New Orleans Times-Picayune*. He was an icon of the civil rights movement and was an internationally known reporter who had covered Mississippi's turbulent racial struggles in the 1960s. L. E. had owned the old Millsaps building in downtown Jackson where Minor's *Times-Picayune* office was located. I had heard L. E. mention Minor on several occasions and knew that the two could not be any farther apart in their views of blacks and the civil rights movement. But I also knew that L. E. had a degree of respect for Minor and had sometimes spoke in a friendly way about him.

Another attendee was Jim Ingram, the Mississippi commissioner of public safety. Jim was a retired FBI agent who worked tirelessly trying to put together criminal cases against L. E., Bowers, and Hawkins. But he and Minor were there to pay their respects. I was trying to wrap my mind around the cast of opposing characters at L. E.'s funeral: violent Klansmen, a civil rights leader, a liberal newspaper reporter dedicated to civil rights, and a hard-nosed FBI agent, all paying their respects. One of the most surreal moments of my life. My family had long-standing ties to Minor. My grandfather had been friends with him, and my brother, Sam, had worked for him at the *Jackson Capital Reporter*, a newspaper that Minor had owned and published between 1977 and 1981. After introducing myself, I said, "Only in Mississippi could this occur, Mr. Minor." He smiled and nodded his head in agreement. A few days later, Minor wrote a *Clarion-Ledger* piece about the funeral and quoted Ingram as saying, "This is the passing of an era." He was right.

I will not say negative things about Dannie, L. E., Sam, or any of my old prison friends. Some had been involved in terrible crimes, but I'm not going to betray them at this point in my life. Instead, I made a deliberate choice to move on from my relationships with them. At that time in my life, I still harbored some of my old beliefs, but they were nothing like the ones I'd had before going to prison, and I and my beliefs were continuing to evolve. I continued to think back to those nights in the Atlanta Penitentiary when I wrote letters for Leon. Changing one's beliefs and convictions is a process, not a burst of blinding light; it takes time and effort. In my case, it took a long time. It happened little by little, day by day and year by year.

My attempts to ditch my previous life were compromised by a couple of articles that appeared in the *Clarion-Ledger*. The first one came out in November 1982, after a reporter, Orley Hood, discovered me while driving through the Beer Barn one afternoon. He told another reporter, and she interviewed me a few weeks later. The article "Bayou of Pigs: Planner Has No Regrets," featured a recent photo of me standing with my arms crossed and wearing the same Bad Bob's T-shirt I'd been photographed in when I was arrested. I looked tough and determined—just what you'd expect a revolutionary to look like.

The two-page article described not only the details of the Dominica plot and its aftermath but also my role in the Klan. It also mentioned my arrest for assaulting two black police officers. The article ended by saying that I was hoping to become a criminal defense lawyer, though I had just begun thinking about the idea and hadn't yet decided that's what I wanted to do. On the whole, the article wasn't bad. The journalist even described me as "polished and articulate" (though she also said that I "moped" about my years of parole). I don't know where she got that. I've never moped in my life. If anyone disapproved of the article, I never heard it—all of the feedback I received was positive. After all, I was no longer a mercenary, a convict, or a Klansman. I was a college student trying to improve his life.

About a year later, the *Clarion-Ledger* published another article on me because the invasion of Grenada was hot news. The article claimed I was upset when I heard about the invasion because the US government had done nearly the same thing that it had sent me to prison for doing. That was a bit of an exaggeration.

I wasn't immune to politics, though. I was still an admirer of George Wallace and identified with his new political stance, which partially recanted his earlier "Segregation Forever" pledge. In 1979, he'd said something along the lines of, "I was wrong. Those days are over and ought to be over." I agreed. The philosophy I'd held in the navy and later in the Klan was no longer relevant or useful. I, too, was moving on.

I mostly focused on school. After my release from prison, I worked seven days a week, an average of about ten hours every day, and I saved enough money to buy an old station wagon. It wasn't a nice car, but it was transportation. And I saved enough to cover a semester's tuition at Hinds Junior College, where I enrolled in the spring of 1983. I wasn't sure what I wanted my major to be. I enjoyed history and writing, so I took a lot of English classes and had some excellent professors in Western Civilization.

Money was an issue, even though I was working two jobs. I wanted to transfer to a four-year college, but wasn't sure how I would manage financially, so I took a semester off to save money. I got a job as a roofer—a hard, physically demanding job.

On my first day of work, I was told to report to the Red Roof Inn under construction in Ridgeland, Mississippi. For the next seven days I worked from daylight to dusk carrying seventy-pound bundles of shingles and staging them on the roof. By the end of the week, I was more convinced than ever that I didn't want to be a low-skilled laborer all my life. But I worked as much as I could and saved enough money to go back to Hinds.

By the end of 1984, I was done at Hinds and had transferred to Belhaven, an expensive private college in Jackson. My grades were exemplary, with several semesters of a perfect 4.0. I wanted to complete my degree as soon as possible, which meant taking more classes each semester and working less. I began taking out student loans and working mostly on weekends.

In an English class at Belhaven, we read Herman Melville's *Bartleby the Scrivener*, and I wrote in a term paper that Bartleby is a misfit, outcast, and radical in a pitiless and unfeeling society. He is prone to speak his mind and to do as he pleases, at least to some extent; also, he seems to reject authority, with little regard for the consequences. I guess I identified with him, and I had paid a steep price for it.

In 1985, I transferred again, this time to the University of Southern Mississippi, which was much more affordable. Originally, I thought I might go to Mississippi State and follow in my father's footsteps by pursuing a degree in engineering, but I chose Southern because it was in the same federal judicial district as Jackson, meaning that I wouldn't have to change parole officers. It may sound odd, but I liked my parole officer, Hugh Parham. He was tough but fair, and I could tell he wanted me to succeed. Mr. Parham had a genuine interest in seeing me do well and had taken notice of my successes and lifestyle changes.

By the time I enrolled at Southern, I had a better idea of who I was. At twenty-five, I felt it was past time for me to get serious about putting my goals into action, and I was ready for my real life to begin. But I still had to decide what my real life would be. Maybe a career as a lawyer was where I was headed, if I could jump the hurdles. And there were a lot of hurdles, most of them of my own making.

I really buckled down, more eager than ever to obtain my degree. I took out student loans and worked part-time doing small remodeling jobs and handyman work to help pay my tuition and living expenses. I also purchased an old, ragged-out mobile home at a trailer park, complete with leaky roof and a family of possums that lived in the ductwork of the defunct central heating/cooling system. The possum family included nine babies that entered the trailer at night through the missing vent covers on the floor. This was their playground and I tried to coexist with them, but sometimes they got into bed with me when I was sleeping, so they had to go. I didn't want to kill them, so I placed few mothballs in the ductwork to encourage them seek out new accommodations; it worked and they moved on, and I slept better at night. After the possums left, I spent a couple of weeks patching up the trailer and made it livable in no time. It wasn't nice by any stretch of the imagination, but it would do for a couple years.

Because of my work demands and school schedule, I had little time for social activities. I made many new friends at Southern who like me were invested in getting an education but also liked to have fun. And because of my experiences in prison, I needed to have fun. Despite my grueling schedule and commitment to education, I was wild at heart. That wild streak was still there even though I knew it might get me into trouble with the law. It did.

Although in some ways I felt old compared to the other college students, in other ways I wanted to make up for the youth I'd lost. While in my second semester at Southern, I attended a party with some school friends from Prentiss, Mississippi. The party was held in an apartment located in a large complex on Highway 49. As college parties often do, it got a little loud. Actually, it got really loud—music blaring and drunken voices hollering well into the early hours of the morning. Eventually other tenants in the complex called the cops to complain.

When the cops showed up at the door, they ordered me and a few others to step outside. I refused because I thought I wouldn't be arrested if I stayed inside the apartment. I was wrong. They pulled me out and arrested me for public drunkenness, even though I hadn't been in public. That argument didn't seem to cut any ice with them. They cuffed my hands behind my back and stuck me in a police car while they returned to the apartment to make more arrests.

When I saw one of my friends, Charlie Speed, walk by, I hollered, "Hey Slick! Open the door!" He wasn't too sober either, so he opened the door of the police car and I bolted, taking off across Highway 49 with my wrists handcuffed behind my back.

Several policemen chased after me, but I had a head start. I cut across four lanes of traffic, dodging the cars and paying no attention to the cops yelling at me to stop. There were dense woods on the other side of the highway, and I ducked my head and ran into them, making my way through the brush to look for a place to hide. I was now in my element. I found a shallow ditch with heavy vegetation growing in and around it. It was a dark night with no moonlight, so I burrowed into the mud in the ditch. I'd found the perfect hiding spot. Someone would literally have to step on me to discover it.

I lay there for at least an hour while the cops searched for me. They avoided the muddy ditch, however, maybe because they thought it was too wet to hide in. I watched the beams of their lights play back and forth on the trees, but they passed me by again and again. It was uncomfortable lying in the mud with my hands behind my back and the steel cuffs biting into my wrists and back, and it got more uncomfortable when the mosquitoes found me. They began lighting on my face and had a feast, but I suffered through. I was pretty sure the cops weren't going to find me if I lay still and quiet enough, and I was right, as they eventually stopped searching and went away.

I stayed there for another hour because I thought they might be waiting for me to come out. Then I eased out of the ditch and made my way to a nearby road. I didn't see any police cars. I crossed at a dark place and walked to a nearby apartment complex where a friend lived, using the edge of the handcuffs to clumsily knock on his door. When he opened it, I pushed my way inside and shoved the door closed with my foot. I was a hell of a sight, and he called some friends of mine who came to get me; they took me to a mobile home just outside of Hattiesburg. I had been drinking beer earlier in the night and by now I had to pee really badly, but with my hands cuffed behind my back I couldn't do it without wetting myself. There were several girls drinking and hanging around, so I paid one of them twenty dollars to unzip my pants and hold my equipment while I urinated.

My friends took me to a guy they thought might have a key to the handcuffs, but he didn't, so they found a metal-cutting chisel and a hammer and I laid my hands on a concrete curb while they cut the chain. My friends were drunk and missed a few times, so my hands and wrists got pretty beat up.

My girlfriend and one of her friends drove me back to my mobile home—a couple of twenty-one-year-old sorority girls who thought that hanging out with an ex-con who had just been arrested and escaped was funny. It stopped being funny the next morning before daylight, however, when the police showed up at my trailer to arrest me. Someone at the party had ratted me out. The same two guys who had arrested me the night before were there to arrest me again. They beat on my door and ordered me outside. I knew the jig was up, so I didn't protest as they dragged me outside, handcuffed me for a second time, and threw me into the police car. They were furious. I had made them look foolish by outrunning and eluding them, so they charged me with escape, resisting arrest, disorderly conduct, abusive language, and, oh yeah, destruction of government property—the handcuffs. Then they threw me in jail.

I posted bond the next day and went to court a month or so later. I hired one of the old Klan attorneys from the 1960s, Travis Buckley, to represent me, but he was in the hospital with a back problem at the time I went to court, so I asked for a continuance. The judge flat-out denied the request, and I had to represent myself. That ended up being kind of fun because I got to cross-examine the two officers who had chased me that night. The black cop was an okay guy, but the white cop was ruthless. He testified that I was "falling down drunk," so when I got my turn to cross-examine him, I said, "If I was so drunk, how did I manage to outrun two police officers and then hide so well that you couldn't find me, even though I had my hands cuffed behind my back and you all had flashlights?" The madder he got, the more I enjoyed toying with him.

Of course I was found guilty. I was sentenced to thirty days in jail and fined a thousand dollars. I had a little money saved up, so I posted an appeals bond immediately and then Travis took my case pro bono. He was a cagey guy and knew how to play the system, and he liked me. For the next five or six years, he kept getting postponements and new court dates until I was finally offered a deal to plead to public drunkenness and they'd dismiss the rest of the charges and expunge the whole thing from my record.

A few weeks after the ditch episode, I met with my parole officer, Mr. Parham, at our monthly appointment. I told him the story straight up and totally honest. He shrugged and didn't seem too concerned. By that time I'd been out on parole for several years and had done well.

The other really wild event I was involved in occurred several months after my arrest and escape. It had snowed in Hattiesburg, with about three or four inches on the ground. I was still driving my old station wagon, which didn't maneuver too well on icy roads, so I stayed in one Friday night with my girlfriend. Later that night, two of my buddies from Prentiss, Trey and Grant, came by my trailer in Grant's four-wheel-drive Bronco. We were always playing pranks on one another and they'd concocted one for me that took it to the extreme.

While we were asleep, Grant went to the window on one side of my trailer and Trey came around to the other window, which was in my bedroom. Grant tied a string of firecrackers to a hatchet, lit the firecrackers, and threw them through one window as Trey tied a string of firecrackers to a shovel and simultaneously threw them through the other. We were awakened to the sound of breaking glass and several hundred firecrackers going off.

Trey and Grant were the only people I knew who would carry a prank this far, so I set out to get even with them. They lived in a trailer in Lamar County about fifteen minutes away; the roads were icy and my car slipped and slid as I drove over to their place, where I found the trailer dark and their vehicles gone. I shut off my lights and went down the road to turn around at a catfish restaurant, about to circle back and exact my revenge, but when I pulled into the lot, I noticed two sets of vehicle tracks in the snow leading to the back of the building. I followed them and found Trey's Celica and Grant's Bronco parked next to each other in the shadows.

Without ever getting out of my station wagon, I took a .357 magnum revolver and pumped three rounds into the windshields of each vehicle. The bullets took out the front windows going in and the back ones going out. We were now even.

I returned home, and Trey and Grant called me laughing shortly thereafter. We went out drinking together the following evening. These experiences didn't slow me down from partying, though I did become a lot more careful and smarter. The arrest and escape adventure ended up being my last run-in with the law. I never shot up another car again either.

I also liked to partake in harmless pranks not nearly as nefarious as escaping from the police or shooting up cars. One such prank involved a good friend of mine, Ken Carraway. Ken lived in a nearby apartment and had an odd habit of clipping his fingernails and placing them in a small pile underneath the couch in his den. When he was watching TV he would reach under the couch and pick up a fingernail clipping and chew on it.

I dropped by one day looking for Ken, but he wasn't home. So I flushed his fingernail pile down the toilet and used his clippers to clip my toenails. I then shaved my toenail clippings down to the same size as his fingernail clippings and placed them under the couch in the same spot where I had found his pile. For the next few weeks, several of us could hardly contain our laughter when Ken would reach under the couch and begin chewing on my toenails.

CHAPTER TWELVE

Settling Down

I was still considering going to law school, so during my first semester at Southern I'd concentrated on subjects like History and English. Learning how to write well would come in handy for a lawyer, I figured.

Perhaps I thought about a legal career because I wanted to change that "pitiless and unfeeling society" I wrote about in my Bartleby paper, particularly the society found in prisons. There just had to be a better way of dealing with misfits. In our criminal justice system I saw firsthand how people who had made mistakes—and sometimes just one small mistake—had little chance of rehabilitation. To survive, many people opted to fit in, and to do that in prison, you had to become a worse person, not a better one. I'd been lucky and had gotten a second chance, and to pay it forward, I wanted others to have a second chance, too. Maybe a law degree would provide me with a way to do that and enable me to find some platform, any platform, that would allow me to have even a minor voice in reforming the system.

But despite my desire to advocate for prisoners and sentencing reform, it soon became obvious to me that my dream of going into law was just that—a dream. There was no guarantee I'd be accepted into law school. I was a convicted felon, an ex-mercenary, an ex-Klansman, and an ex-con, after all. I enjoyed English and History, but a degree in English doesn't always get you very far. And the law school dream wasn't my only one. My real passion, which

I'd had for as long as I could remember, was rivers, creeks, woods, swamps, and wildlife.

I recalled a major fish kill in the Pearl River that flowed through my grandfather's land at Hopewell. Filtrol, an industrial plant located about forty river miles upriver, had discharged a massive amount of sulfuric acid when I was in my preteen years. The acid discharge had occurred during very low flow conditions and had killed fish for many miles south of Jackson, virtually wiping out all of the aquatic life in a large segment of my beloved river. Seeing the thousands and thousands of dead fish had sickened and shocked me. I asked my father how this could happen, and he explained that environmental controls were very lax. He, too, was appalled and nauseated by the enormity of it.

The incident had really affected me. I never forgot how I felt while standing on the riverbank at Hopewell, looking into the wild and wonderful place where I had fished and swum and played and seeing it littered with rotting carcasses.

Out of both practicality and passion, I decided to major in environmental studies within the Geography Department. The field was growing, and career possibilities were mushrooming. I wasn't a tree hugger or one of those "snotty-nosed kids" (that's what my dad called them while he was an engineer working on the Alaska pipeline) who protested any kind of development. But I *was* in favor of clean water and clean air. In spite of my past association with the sort of right-wing politics that sometimes raged against governmental "interference" or environmental controls, I believed strongly that some kind of regulatory framework needed to protect the environment from pollution and chemical spills. Even before the 1989 *Exxon Valdez* spill awakened everyone to the dangers of an underregulated industry, I was passionate about protecting our wild spaces. I'd lived behind gray walls and knew how ugly it was.

Declaring my new major led me to a great piece of luck—I was able to study under Professor Bob Wales, who became one of my most important mentors. Dr. Wales managed a number of environmental study grants and was active in the Lamar County Soil and Water Conservation District, and he helped me get a part-time job as an intern with them. I assisted the full-time staff who worked with companies and individuals having difficulties with pollution caused by runoff from various agricultural or forestry practices, providing them with advice about how to minimize those problems. I had no regulatory or enforcement responsibilities. Instead, I gathered information and occasionally made recommendations about best practices.

Dr. Wales later was instrumental in helping me acquire another internship at the Bureau of Marine Resources (now the Department of Marine Resources) within the Mississippi Department of Wildlife and Fisheries. I spent two summers obtaining valuable on-the-job training. I worked up and down the Mississippi Gulf Coast, interviewing commercial and recreational boaters, filling out forms, and then compiling them for the bureau. I ran into some hard cases with a few of the oystermen and shrimpers who really—and I mean *really*—resented any government pukes telling them what they could and could not do. I had no regulatory duties, but that didn't matter to many of the commercial fishermen. I guess they thought they could intimidate a college boy. Of course, I'd worked with and gotten cooperation from a lot tougher guys in prison, so a few crusty old shrimpers weren't going to stop me.

My role was gathering information, and I was good at talking as well as listening. These internships strengthened my belief that reasonable rules and regulations were necessary and needed to be enforced, and my experiences certainly steered me toward an environmental regulatory career.

I never made any attempts to hide my past, but I didn't trumpet it, either. I had lived my whole life in Jackson, which is a tight-knit community, so many people knew who I was and what I'd done. My prison and Klan past was whispered about but rarely seemed to make any difference to the people I hung out with, either my friends or my work associates. This was before the Google age, of course, and the twenty-four-hour news cycle.

But sometimes my past would come back and make a minor splash. In November 1986, the University of Southern Mississippi newspaper heard about me and ran an article recounting in detail the Dominica episode and sharing my feelings about our prison system. I liked how the article began: the student reporter called me "clean-cut, wearing a button-down shirt" and not looking like someone who'd try to overthrow a foreign government. She also highlighted my outstanding academic record and how I was a member of several different honor societies. Even so, I could have done without the notoriety.

In 1987, I reached the end of my six-year sentence. Mr. Parham and I had become relatively close for a parolee and parole officer. He had seen me evolve over four and a half years into a new and much different man than I'd been fresh out of prison. He recommended that my conviction be set aside, which was allowable under the Federal Youth Corrections Act. A few months later, the US Probation Office concurred. It was the highlight of my life to that point, opening the door for me to pursue a professional career without the stigma and restrictions of a convicted felon.

The *Jackson Clarion-Ledger* ran an update on me after my conviction was officially set aside, but the piece wasn't as complimentary as the one in the college paper. In addition to rehashing the Bayou of Pigs fiasco, the article highlighted my Klan past and quoted my high school history teacher referring to me as a "bush-league Charles Manson." I still have no idea what he meant by that, and I've wondered if he ever really said it. I was not going to hide or lie about my past, but I hoped that someday it would become less important when compared to my accomplishments.

A month later I graduated from USM with honors, having made the Dean's List or President's List many semesters despite working the whole time I was in school. I had also accumulated a significant amount of student loan debt and would spend the next ten years paying it off. Today I look at myself as proof that a college degree is entirely possible for an economically disadvantaged student. With hard work, determination, and student loan assistance, I believe anyone can obtain a degree if they want it badly enough.

After graduation I did a semester of graduate school while working as a handyman and then took another internship, this time with the Mississippi Emergency Management Agency (MEMA). That's where "real life" finally began.

MEMA serves as a clearinghouse, coordinating the state's response to various emergencies. For environmental emergencies, MEMA worked with the Department of Environmental Quality (DEQ), the state equivalent of the US Environmental Protection Agency. As a MEMA intern, I was exposed to the various kinds of environmental crises happening around the state, and many of them brought back memories of the Filtrol fish kill that had affected me so greatly. MEMA exposed me to other things as well, including the woman who became my wife.

Diane had worked at MEMA in a number of capacities for several years by the time I arrived. When I came on board, she was the training coordinator. We were almost immediately attracted to each other, even though in many ways we were opposites. I had a wild reputation, and she was totally straight. She'd never gotten drunk— not once. She was a regular churchgoer who seldom missed a Sunday service. She never even cursed. When she was really put out, she might say *darn*, but nothing stronger.

She was also very pretty and, more important, super smart. She had a degree from Mississippi State in mathematics. She came from an educated family—her three sisters also held degrees in mathematics, and her brother was an attorney. Diane's mother was an English teacher at Hinds Junior College, and her father, Rex McRaney, was a prominent banker and lawyer. He had been a vocal proponent of civil rights in the 1960s and had been instrumental in bringing Head Start to Mississippi. He was a good man, and we got along well. Diane was interested in making a difference with her life. All of these things appealed to me.

Diane liked my sense of humor. I was always a big joker, and she liked to laugh. She knew, as everyone seemed to, about my past, but she didn't hold it against me. She didn't like my previous Klan association and thought the Dominica invasion plot was pretty crazy, but she recognized that I was no longer that person. Probably the thing that most drew us together is that we were at the same stage of life. We weren't kids any longer; we were starting our careers and looking to settle down and have a family. We offered each other a chance to fill the gaps in our lives.

Diane was also a help to me in my career. Because she'd been at MEMA for a few years, she had contacts at DEQ. She also had a brother-in-law, Ronnie Robertson, who had been a respected state legislator. In the South, as elsewhere, it always helps to know people who know people. So when she heard about a job opening at DEQ, I applied to become an environmental technician. Ronnie made a few calls on my behalf, and I got the job.

Shortly before my move to DEQ, Diane and I got married, which surprised a lot of people, since I had never been one to settle down. We had a big wedding, and among those who came was my old mentor, Sam Bowers, whom I hadn't seen in quite some time. He gave us a Bible for a wedding present. I didn't see Sam again until 1993 at L. E. Matthews's funeral, which was the last time I ever saw him. (In 1998, Sam was convicted of murder in the 1966 firebombing that killed civil rights leader Vernon Dahmer. Following his conviction, I learned that he was being temporarily held in the Simpson County jail. I traveled to Mendenhall, where he was being held, and dropped off two books for him: a Bible and a book on the French Revolution, which was a favorite subject of his. A jailer offered to let me in to see "Mr. Sam," but I declined. He died in prison in 2006.)

Our honeymoon was pretty spartan. We had no extra money at all—none. I was existing on a student intern salary, which was pitiful, and Diane didn't make much money either. So instead of going to Mexico or the Caribbean, we borrowed Dr. Kenny Williams's beach cottage in Ocean Springs. We couldn't afford to eat out or play. We watched the sun come up and go down.

One day, we used Dr. Williams's small boat with an outboard motor and set off for Horn Island, one of the barrier islands off the coast of Mississippi. I wanted to share my love of fishing with Diane, but the outboard died about a mile off the island, and I had to use the top of an ice chest as a paddle. Horn is remote and uninhabited, part of a national park, and although it has a ranger station somewhere, we didn't know where it was. After we'd spent a couple of hours, wondering how we'd get back to the mainland, a fisherman came along and towed us home. I thought the whole thing was a fun adventure, but Diane didn't agree with me.

I never imagined that twenty-two years later I would return to Horn Island as a leader of a massive cleanup effort to one of the world's worst oil spills.

My marriage to Diane was a watershed moment in my life. She gave me stability, and the wild ways of my past became just that—a part of my past. My life was definitely coming together, just as I had promised myself it would that first morning at Tallahassee Federal Correctional Institute.

CHAPTER THIRTEEN

Making a Difference

My first "real" job in my chosen profession had finally begun. I was twenty-nine years old and more than ready.

The Mississippi Department of Environmental Quality (DEQ) protects the state's natural resources and enforces pollution control laws. Some people might see irony in an ex-con right-winger working for a government regulatory agency, but not me: I was still against unnecessary laws infringing on personal freedom, but it had long been evident to me that reasonable regulations were necessary to have a healthy environment. I figured I could make a difference. My experiences had taught me a lot, and maybe they would even help. They had certainly made me tough.

DEQ is an umbrella agency with several different bureaus: Pollution Control, Land and Water Resources, Geology, and Administrative Services. My first job was as a senior environmental technician in the Bureau of Land and Water Resources, and my primary duties involved issuing permits for irrigation wells. After working for a few months at Land and Water doing mundane tasks, I became very bored, so when a lower-level position opened up in the Bureau of Pollution Control, I jumped at it—even though I had to take a 10 percent reduction in pay—from twenty thousand dollars to eighteen thousand annually. Diane was not at all happy about the pay cut, but doing little more than issuing permits made me restless. I've never been good at handling boredom, and I'd certainly had my fill of it in prison. I needed a position that was more challenging.

My new job was basically as a water pollution inspector. My initial investigations may seem small, but they had an impact on the environment—and on me. I performed compliance inspections on wastewater treatment plants and investigated incidents involving the illegal disposal of waste products, which can damage fragile aquatic ecosystems as well as mammals and birds. I frequently investigated raw sewage discharges that were going directly into state waters—usually a result of mechanical failures or operators choosing to deliberately bypass treatment systems.

I didn't do this alone, of course. I worked with some great people, one of whom was Gloria Tatum. When I started at DEQ, Gloria worked as a chemist in the lab that performed testing on many of the samples I brought in. She was and is very good at her job and didn't put up with any bull. Luckily, she had a sense of humor that matched my own, and we clicked immediately. I gave her crap, and she shoveled it right back at me. Then we'd both laugh. Sometimes lab work and fieldwork can be tedious, but we made it fun.

Soil samples are not glamorous—in fact, they're typically pretty nasty. Sometimes I'd come into the lab covered in mud and prop my boots on the receptionist's desk while she turned up her nose at the smell. Sometimes I'd run out of sample jars in the field and use whatever was handy: one time, I used a discarded mayonnaise jar I'd found buried in a dumpsite. It frustrated Gloria and the other workers, but when working in the field, you sometimes run out of supplies and have to make do.

Gloria gave me another nickname, one I'm not sure I liked better than Huck. Because I often forgot to wipe my muddy boots, she started calling me Mudvaney. I got even with her, though. After we'd known each other a while, I gave her a nickname, but she would kill me if I made it public. Every time I said it, she'd laugh.

Gloria is black. We had known each other for just a few months when I told her about my prison experience, and even about my brief stint in the KKK. I just put it out there.

"I have something I need to share with you," I said one morning when I walked into her lab.

"Oh my God, what now?" she asked, laughing. I guess she figured I was about to tell her another joke.

"A long time ago, I was a Klansman."

"Say what?"

"It was a long time ago. I was young, but yeah, I was a Klansman. I also spent some time in prison. I got out at age twenty-two and never looked back."

There was a short silence, and then she said, "Okay, so what do you want me to do about it?"

"Well, I just wanted you to know. I didn't want you to hear it from someone else. I like you and trust you and I don't want to betray our friendship."

Gloria shrugged. "Listen, you goof. I don't know all you did, and I'm not happy about it, but you admitting to this when you didn't have to tells me that you can be trusted. I trust you a lot more than some white people who pretend they're not racist."

And that was that. Gloria and I have remained friends for almost thirty years. She worked herself up the ladder at DEQ from chemist to division director of field services and then environmental justice coordinator, both of which are very senior positions. Today, Gloria is one of my closest confidants. Sometimes I still call her by her old nickname, and she still laughs.

I was active in a conservation organization, the Mississippi Wildlife Federation, which was popular with hunters and fishermen, and was asked to write an article for their monthly magazine, *Mississippi Wildlife*. My six-page article, "A Day in the Life of a Pollution Investigator," was published in October 1990.

While I was a tougher inspector than most that I worked with, I prided myself on being fair. I always went the extra mile to find the source of surface water pollution even though it sometimes involved great persistence and dedication. Most of the companies

and citizens I encountered wanted a clean environment and com-
plied with regulations, but there were others who knew little about
how their practices hurt the environment, and many of them didn't
care much, either. This really bothered me. I was starting to get a
name within DEQ—a good one this time, one that I could be proud
of. I was becoming known as someone who did not like to give up,
someone who showed a dogged persistence in nosing out polluters.
My boss said, "George is like a pit bull. He just never lets go."

In early 1990, I moved from the water pollution team to DEQ's
emergency response team. We rolled out whenever there was a natural disaster, oil spill, chemical spill, landfill fire, chemical/oil fire,
or a hazardous waste spill as well as whenever the DEQ discovered environmentally criminal activities such as illegal disposal of
hazardous waste. The Emergency Services Branch had only three
employees, including my boss, Bob Rogers. Bob had been in the
emergency response business for many years and was a wealth of
knowledge. He was definitely old school, but overall he was a good
guy as well as a walking encyclopedia of spill response.

The state provided me with a four-wheel-drive pickup truck with
a flashing emergency light on top, a two-way radio, and a pager—
high-tech for 1990. A couple of years later, we were issued cellular
phones. It was one of the old bag phones that wasn't very porta-
ble outside of the truck, but it revolutionized communications for
us. When on call, I responded to whatever emergency came into
our office, and when I arrived at the emergency site, I was the law.
Another irony.

I liked this job for a number of reasons: I loved nature and
protecting our environment, I loved adventure, and I hated irre-
sponsible people—especially those who lied or wouldn't own up to
what they'd done. And when I encountered chronic environmental
polluters or those with a total disregard for their actions, I made it
my mission to make them face their own music. Fortunately, these
kinds of people were the exception to the rule, but make no mistake,
there were plenty of them out there in the early 1990s.

It was my job to assess the damage and then oversee the cleanup performed by whoever was responsible for the incident. When there was no identifiable responsible party or when someone was financially unable to pay for the cleanup, DEQ would hire the contractor to perform the necessary services.

Cleanups weren't always easy. Sometimes they were adversarial, and I encountered deception, feigned ignorance, and outright lies. I had many battles with some hard cases. Some were outright defiant and attempted to intimidate and threaten me. They didn't know my history; plus, now I had the law on my side and I was in the right.

The first oil spill I worked was a good example of a company that had total disregard for the environment. There was a report of oil in a creek outside of Natchez, so Bob and I drove down there together. Before we left Jackson, Bob had hired a contractor to contain the oil since there was no known responsible party. When we arrived, we met the contractor at the downstream point where the oil was contained. Bob and I followed the oil upstream for about a mile until we came to a steep embankment on one side of the creek where a residual trail of oil led up the hill.

I climbed the hill while Bob stayed at the creek bed below; at the crest, I found an oil-field service company. There was a rack where trucks came in to be washed, and it was apparent that a tank truck had come in, backed up to the wash rack, and dumped a load of waste crude oil.

I went inside the building, identified myself, and asked to see the manager. The receptionist escorted me back to an office where I met the owner, whom I'll call Sean.

"What can I do for you, Mr. Malvaney?" he asked.

"We're investigating an oil spill in the creek. We followed the oil upstream about a mile, and it stops at the bottom of the hill below your wash rack."

"Nah, it's not us," he said confidently.

"I need you to come down to the creek with me to talk to my boss," I replied.

Nervously shuffling papers around his desk, Sean said in an agitated voice, "I'm really busy and don't have time to fool with something that doesn't concern us." He refused to look me in the eye. It was all too obvious that he badly wanted to avoid coming down to the creek with me.

I was new to this game: this was my first oil spill, and I wasn't sure what I could or should do to get him to come with me. So I boldly replied, "Well, we will immediately initiate an enforcement case against you and will be seeking twenty-five thousand dollars a day in fines plus the cost of the cleanup if you don't cooperate." At this point he turned and looked directly at me, and we locked eyes for a moment. I never blinked and my face was expressionless. Sean knew I meant business and wasn't backing down. He agreed to come down to the creek where Bob was waiting.

We worked our way down the hill, and Sean stood in the creek bed, looked up at the hill where his wash rack was, and repeated, "Nah, it didn't come from us." Bob pointed out that there was no oil up the creek from where we were, only downstream, but Sean continued to deny it. Then we heard a truck's air brakes screech. About two minutes later, a torrent of crude oil and water cascaded down the hill and into the creek, right where we were standing.

Bob stuck his finger in the water and tasted it. "Salt water," he said (When oil wells pump crude oil out of the ground, saltwater often comes up with the oil. Normally, the oil and saltwater are separated, and the saltwater is then injected back into the ground.) Sean took off running up the hill as fast as he could. He had a head start on me, but I followed him and heard him swearing under his breath. When we got to the top, the swearing grew louder as we both saw a giant vacuum tanker backed up to the wash rack with its tail valve open.

"Goddamn it, DEQ is right behind me," I heard him say, but then he saw me standing there and mumbled something about his drivers going against his policies. He shrugged. We'd caught him red-handed, not only dumping oil but bald-faced lying about it.

We fined the company ten thousand dollars, and they also had to pay for the cleanup. Today they would probably face criminal charges as well as a much larger fine. The oil production business at the time was having difficulties—crude oil was down to less than twenty dollars a barrel, so many major oil companies were getting out of production in Mississippi. They were selling off their fields, and small independent outfits had popped up to take advantage of the cheap prices. Some of these guys cared nothing about the environment and were only interested in making a quick buck.

I didn't like what I saw that day. They didn't care, and it made me angry. This isn't to say that all small independent oil producers were environmental outlaws while all large producers were stewards of the environment, but the percentage of outlaws among the smaller independents was disproportionately high.

The attitude of Sean and others like him made me more determined to get my sites as clean as possible, as close to the natural conditions before the spill occurred. This set me apart from some of my counterparts. Regulators had the power to decide what was clean and what was not, and others had different, and looser, standards than I did. They might say, "You got most of it, we'll let the next rain do the rest," and let the cleanup stop. Not me. As long as residual surface oil or oil-saturated debris remained, I always said, "Keep going." I began to get a reputation as a hard-nosed regulator. I pushed and pushed some more to get all of the surface oil removed—not 90 percent of it, *all* of it.

One time I dealt with a contractor in South Mississippi who cleaned up spills for private companies. He hired game wardens who needed extra money as laborers. This contractor was cleaning up a spill in a small creek in a remote area of Franklin County with extremely difficult access. When I went to inspect, I saw small amounts of residual surface oil remaining as they moved downstream. I advised them to go back upstream and recover every bit of it.

"Why do you make us clean to this high standard when none of the others do?" asked Tub, a big guy who was one of the game wardens. He wasn't being combative; he was curious.

I explained that I was the only line of defense between the environment and the pollution, and I wanted to get it back to as close to its natural state as possible: "There wasn't oil in this creek before the spill, and there shouldn't be any after the cleanup." And if it cost the company extra money, that was the cost of doing business. The game wardens and other contractors as well as the oil companies began to notice that when I was at a site it took longer to clean spills. What might have taken five to seven days under another regulator might take ten days when I was there.

I took a lot of pride in my work. I didn't sit in my truck like some regulators did. Instead, I walked every inch of a spill up and down, up and down, until it was clean (and some spills went many miles through rough terrain with no roads—just briars, underbrush, and venomous snakes). When the contractor was shorthanded, I would jump in and help as if I was one of the crew.

The bottom line was that I took these things personally. I didn't like what I saw happening, and my response was to work even harder and levy more penalties when gross negligence or deliberate acts were involved. To be clear, when a responsible oil company (which most are) had a spill that was not a result of gross negligence or a deliberate act and was aggressively seeking to clean up the mess, I never pursued monetary penalties. Spills are a cost of the production of crude oil, and I did not and do not believe in penalizing companies that act responsibly and prudently.

Soon after I joined the Emergency Services Branch, a fish kill occurred on the Pearl River near Hopewell. Of course, it reminded me of the one that had so upset me when I was a child. But this time, I was in a regulatory role, trying to determine the cause and prevent further damage. A biologist from the Department of Wildlife, Fisheries, and Parks and I launched our boat at Rockport and motored up the river, collecting water samples as dead fish floated by. Soon, we were immediately below my old family cabin, and at that instant I knew without a doubt that I'd found my purpose in life.

Before I arrived, DEQ had a reactive strategy, waiting for a spill to be reported and then looking for the culprit. I proactively searched for places where I suspected there might be spills, driving around oil fields operated by known environmental outlaws and looking for spills from flow lines or storage tanks. Such "pollution patrols" were very unpopular in the oil patch, but they were effective. So of course, the outlaw operators hated the patrols; oddly enough, so did one of our sister state agencies, the Mississippi State Oil and Gas Board.

I also developed a small network of snitches who would call me when they had knowledge of a spill that had not been reported. These snitches were usually managers at oilfield service companies that performed roustabout services in the oil patch. I caught a few of them in some relatively minor environmental infractions, and then worked out a deal with them where I wouldn't pursue monetary penalties if they agreed to contact me confidentially and report spills.

These aggressive techniques resulted in the discovery of many unreported spills, and I went hard after the responsible parties. I wasn't always popular, but I began to see a noticeable difference in the oil fields of south Mississippi, particularly in the Natchez, Waynesboro, and Laurel areas, where a disproportionate number of outlaws operated. The improvements were significant and I was proud of the fact that I was making a difference.

The oil patch certainly didn't have a monopoly on environmental outlaws. Back in the 1990s, it wasn't uncommon to encounter midnight dumpings of hazardous waste in remote locations. Toxic hazardous waste is much easier to hide than oil, which makes itself known pretty fast. Hazardous waste can be buried for years and present absolutely no visible evidence of its presence. Buried hazardous waste became my specialty.

One of my first run-ins with buried hazardous waste was memorable and still gets talked about more than twenty years later. It started in the way most of these cases did—with an anonymous tip. Like many anonymous tips, this one was vague. The caller said that there were buried pesticides at the Magee Farm Cooperative but gave no specifics about what was buried or where. An inspector of DEQ's Solid Waste Division performed the initial investigation but was unable to substantiate the claim and turned it over to me.

I went down to the co-op and interviewed the manager, whom I'll call Sam Michaels. Michaels was a smug, middle-aged man with a superior attitude. When I told him we'd had a complaint about buried pesticides, he denied any knowledge. When I asked if I could look around, he shrugged and said, "Go ahead. I don't care." His attitude wasn't friendly or unfriendly, but I had a gut feeling there was something going on and that he knew something about it. I didn't see anything that might indicate chemicals had been buried, but I'd learned to trust my gut. I had to leave to investigate a diesel spill south of Magee, and when I was on my way back, I went by the Co-Op again, pulling up to the fuel pump in my DEQ truck. While I filled up, I chatted with a few employees milling around the gas station. Then I walked across the street to the main building and talked with a couple of other employees. I sensed that some of them were angry, which made me all the more suspicious. I made one last pass through the grounds looking for something—anything—that might indicate a possible burial site, but I found nothing. When I returned to my truck, a folded piece of paper was stuck under the driver's side wiper blade. I casually took it off and drove several blocks up the road where I stopped and unfolded it: *If you want to know where the chemicals are buried, come back here tonight right after dark and meet me behind the gas station.*

I knew that I should report this to my boss; I also knew that if I did, upper management at DEQ would order me not to return. I wondered if I was being set up for something dangerous. Possibly, but what the hell.

That night, I pulled into the closed gas station, stuck a .357 magnum revolver under my belt, got out of my truck, and walked around back. It was a still night with very little moonlight and no breeze, eerily quiet with only the sound of gravel crunching under my boots, crickets and some road noise from Highway 49 off in the distance. I could make out a stand of bushes and small trees not too far from where I stood, so I eased over toward them. At that moment, a voice from the bushes told me to come closer. I didn't recognize the voice but figured it must be one of the employees I'd spoken to earlier, perhaps even the original anonymous complainant.

"There's chemicals buried in the old grain crusher," said the voice. I could vaguely make out the dark figure of the man, partially obscured by the bushes. An arm appeared and pointed to a wide-open area not far from where we were standing.

"That was an old grain crusher before we tore it down. There was water in the basement before we filled it in," he went on. "Michaels told us to dump a bunch of drums of pesticides in there, and then he took a shotgun and shot the drums so they'd sink. Then we hauled in truckloads of soil and covered it up." Before I could ask any questions, he said, "Gotta go," and I heard rustling as he ducked out of the bush and scuttled away. I didn't try to follow him. I never saw his face or learned who he was.

I didn't know what to do next. The area in question was approximately twenty by forty feet and, according to the guy in the bush, as deep as twenty feet. Sifting through the area to find a few drums would require a large excavator. But I couldn't go to the DEQ attorneys to get an order to perform an expensive subsurface search on the word of an anonymous figure hiding behind a bush. And I felt certain that if I asked Michaels to voluntarily bring in earth-moving equipment to uncover the drums, he would simply deny that they were there and refuse to do it.

I spent the entire ninety-minute drive home thinking about how to investigate but couldn't come up with anything. Then, BOOM! A plan flashed into my mind. The diesel spill south of Magee needed to have contaminated soil removed from a roadside ditch. It wasn't a big spill, so normally we would have brought in a rubber-tired backhoe, a rather small piece of earth-moving equipment that was not sufficient for exploring the grain crusher area. But I could use that spill to get a large, tracked excavator that could do both jobs. I contacted Riedel-Peterson Environmental Services in Jackson and instructed them to mobilize a two-man crew to the diesel spill south of Magee but to bring an excavator rather than a backhoe.

When the guy asked why we needed a large excavator for such a small spill, I said, "Just bring it."

The next day, while the crew was digging up the contaminated soil along the highway, I went up to the Co-Op and met with Michaels in his office. He was obviously irritated that someone from DEQ had come to ask him about buried chemicals for a third time.

"Now what?" he asked.

"I have obtained information that there are drums of chemicals buried across the street. I'm going to bring in a piece of equipment this evening to dig a few test holes. If we don't find anything, that will conclude my investigation and I won't be back."

I was trying to get Michaels to think that the DEQ investigation would be over if we didn't find anything, but what I was actually saying is that *my* investigation would be over and *I* would not be returning. I intended to turn the case over to the Hazardous Waste Division and let them pursue it.

Michaels gave me his smug look again and said, "Do whatever you want. I don't care. There's nothing there. You're not going to find anything."

I couldn't justify the cost of bringing the crew back a second day, that evening was my only chance. I wouldn't have much time to do the exploratory digging—maybe just enough time to dig a couple of test holes. The odds of hitting the exact spot where the drums were buried were small, but the informant had said that Michaels shot holes in some of the containers. I would also collect soil and water samples to be analyzed for agricultural chemicals: if any were detected, we would have the evidence we needed to perform a thorough site investigation.

When the contractors arrived with the excavator, I rushed them to get it unloaded and begin digging: we only had a couple hours of daylight left. I directed them to dig a hole at each end of the grain crusher, knowing it was a long shot that we'd find anything with just two of them. It was like searching for the proverbial needle in a haystack.

The operator was a young man, Glen Thompson. He had just begun digging when I noticed him stop and reverse. I started to get aggravated—every second counted. "Damn, Glen, we need to be digging," I said to myself. Then it hit me. A strong odor burned my nostrils in spite of the air-purifying respirator I was wearing. I circled around for a better view. Protruding out of the soil in the excavator bucket was the top half of a drum with a thick orange-red liquid oozing from it. The first test hole had dug right down on a drum! We dug several more buckets of soil and recovered two or three more drums. Sometimes you just get lucky.

Sam Michaels didn't share our luck that day. I went into his office to tell him that we'd found the drums and that I was bringing in supplies and more crew. I'd called the fire department and police department because of the foul chemical smell permeating the area. It was amazing how fast that smug look left his face; he stammered and said he didn't know what was in those drums or how they got there.

Our formal site investigation lasted many months, and in the end we discovered a total of twenty-nine drums of insecticides, including Dinoseb, which can cause reproductive difficulties, and azinphos-methyl, which can damage the nervous system. Several containers had deteriorated so much that all of their contents had leaked out and we couldn't read the labeling; laboratory analysis detected 2,4,5-Trichlorophenoxyacetic acid (a defoliant that is the primary ingredient in Agent Orange) and others, most of them banned by the EPA.

The FBI became involved, and I worked closely with the special agent assigned to the case, Bill Baumgartner, as well as the US Attorney's Office. Michaels eventually pled guilty to federal charges related to illegal disposal of regulated hazardous wastes. I was and still am proud of my role in this case (now known as the Burning Bush), which would never have been discovered if I hadn't been persistent and creative. I became known as a guy who never gave up and who solved many cases involving buried or illegally disposed of hazardous waste. I spent many weekends and holidays responding to environmental emergencies, which meant that Diane was home alone dealing with our two toddlers, Forrest, who was born in December 1990, and Hillary, who came along one year later. Despite the demands Diane faced, she rarely complained.

Although we were living paycheck to paycheck, with no money for vacations or luxuries, we did scrape up enough money to go in with a few other people to purchase a fish camp near Thornton, Mississippi. It was an old mobile home sitting on Bee Lake, which is an oxbow lake of the Yazoo River. Each of the four owners had their own bedroom. Ours was in an addition that became known as the Rat Room because the rats seemed to use it as their point of entry and exit. We could hear them scampering through the ceiling and squealing inside the walls. Every now and then they would run across the bed while we were sleeping. As much as she hated them (which was a lot), Diane dealt with the rats, too.

The Bee Lake camp became our weekend getaway. We hunted ducks in the winter and fished in the spring, summer, and fall. We ran trotlines, jug-fished, frog-gigged, barbecued, drank beer, and enjoyed just getting away. I had been taking Forrest hunting since he was about three and had him target shooting by the time he was five, so when we got the Bee Lake camp, he loved it. Hillary soon learned to run jugs for catfish and developed a taste for grilled wild game. When she was about six, I killed a couple of coons at Bee Lake. I barbecued them on the grill and she absolutely loved them, boasting that her favorite food was "barbecued coon." For years afterward, she often asked for it. To this day, Hillary has a real affinity for barbecued coon. Diane never got quite used to the Rat Room, but she, too, enjoyed going to the lake and grilling out or reading on the porch. But when the weekend was over, it was back to work for both of us.

Not too far from the camp at Bee Lake is the town of Greenwood, and just outside of Greenwood is Six Mile Lake, located near the town of Money. In the mid-1990s, I was sent to the lake to investigate a complaint that someone had dumped huge loads of fish entrails and fish heads into the lake. A powerful state senator, Bunky Huggins, chair of the Appropriations Committee, had a cabin there and wasn't happy about dead fish stinking up his retreat. Nobody knew who was doing the dumping, so DEQ executive director Jimmy Palmer dispatched me to catch someone in the act.

"Malvaney," he said, "I don't care how you do it, but get up there and find whoever is doing this. And don't come back until you do."

When I arrived, a local gave me a tour, and I saw more than a thousand rotting fish carcasses. It was evident that whoever was doing this was dumping very large volumes—not just a few fishermen throwing out the remains of their daily catch. This was clearly the work of a large-scale commercial fish-processing operation.

I suspected that the waste was being dumped from a bridge that crossed the lake. Parking my truck some distance away, I hiked down to the bank and hid in the heavy vegetation where I had a good view of the bridge above. I spent two days hunkered down with a video camera. The first day no one dumped anything. In the late afternoon of the second day, however, a large truck stopped in the middle of the bridge and I turned on my camera. Two men emerged from the truck and dumped fifty-five-gallon drum after fifty-five-gallon drum of fish waste into the lake—fish heads and guts cascading down directly in front of me. The smell was overpowering.

Then came the real excitement. I have no idea why, but the men threw a television off the bridge. It floated on the surface, so one of the men got a gun and began shooting at the TV, evidently trying to sink it. The bullets were striking just a few yards in front of me, which was a bit unnerving, and every time they fired, I flinched. When Jimmy Palmer saw the video I brought back, he roared with laughter every time the camera jumped. Jimmy and I still get a kick out of that. The following week, I served a cease-and-desist order on the commercial fishing operation and ordered them to properly dispose of the waste at a landfill.

Many of the cases I worked on during the 1990s were dangerous, although more to the environment than to me personally. I worked on spills of various toxic chemicals from train derailments, tanker truck wrecks, and chemical warehouse fires as well as old, unstable explosives found in the unlikeliest of places. I got well acquainted with people in the FBI, Bureau of Alcohol, Tobacco, and Firearms, US Attorney's Office, Mississippi Attorney General's Office, and numerous other state and federal agencies.

Despite the seriousness of the cases I typically worked, there were sometimes instances of humor. One time, my co-worker, Kevin Posey, and I were investigating a report of Agent Orange buried by a large timber company near Baxterville. We drove almost three hours from our office to interview a former company employee, but when we got to his house, he'd already left for work. While we were waiting for him to get off work, we decided to drive to a nearby oil field and look for unreported spills or other violations. We pulled into an oil exploration company's tank battery site located on the banks of Clear Creek, a beautiful and aptly named stream with a sand and gravel bed. Immediately behind the tank battery was a large pool of water where the creek channel widened and deepened.

Kevin spied a school of bass in the water and came back to get me. I kept fishing tackle in my DEQ truck, so we pulled out a couple of rods. I went upstream and Kevin downstream on either side of a briar patch to get into locations that would allow us to cast. I was working my way around the briars when I heard Kevin holler, "Get over here quick!"

As I approached, I could see what was obviously crude oil flowing downstream. "What the hell happened?"

"I was trying to cast and stepped on a flow line and it broke," Kevin replied.

The flow line was old and deteriorated, and although it was no longer active, it still had a significant amount of residual oil inside it.

Since there was nothing we could do to stop it, we jumped into my truck and sped to the oil company's field office. "Damn it, y'all have a broken flow-line pouring oil directly into Clear Creek! We were inspecting your tank battery and discovered the leak," I hollered.

They immediately sprang into action, and we helped them deploy boom to contain it before it could have any significant effect. The manager of the production company was very thankful that we had discovered the spill so early. Years later, we finally 'fessed up, and although we saw no humor in the incident at the time, now we get a chuckle out of it.

And later that day, we caught up with the former timber company employee and got his information about the buried chemicals. We eventually found the drums, which didn't contain Agent Orange but nevertheless had herbicides that had been banned by the EPA. We also discovered that the toxic chemicals had gotten into a nearby well and that a local family had been drinking the water for years.

Some of the cases I've investigated have generated a lot of interest from the press and the general public. One particularly notable incident took place in the mid-1990s and involved a Louisiana company that was picking up infectious biological waste from that state's Department of Health Laboratory and abandoning it in Pike County rather than sending the waste for incineration. Two other cases that occurred at around the same time in Pike County involved illegal disposal of hazardous chemical waste. Ernest Herndon, an avid outdoorsman and a reporter for the *McComb Enterprise-Journal*, covered the stories and wrote an editorial in which he dubbed me the DEQ Sleuth.

I may have had a good reputation with the public, but for some in the regulated community, I was becoming known as a pain in the ass. And others in the agency felt that my aggressive techniques made them look bad. Nevertheless, I generally had the support of my boss, Bob Rogers, as well as his bosses, Charles Chisolm and Jimmy Palmer, even though my actions occasionally put us all in the hot seat.

Not surprisingly, my biggest detractors were oil producers who didn't like my hard-nosed approach or the monetary penalties I pushed when I uncovered their illegalities or blatant disregard for the environment. The oil industry has a lot of clout in Mississippi, and it used its political pressure against me. Industry executives complained loudly to the Oil and Gas Board and other state agencies and to elected officials, putting pressure on Jimmy to move me somewhere else. (Palmer defended me and refused to transfer me out of their hair. He did, however, counsel me on how to "tone it down" a bit from time to time.) I went head-to-head with the director of the Oil and Gas Board and clashed with the board's field inspectors, who were notorious for defending outlaw operators. Field inspectors frequently attempted to disrupt my investigations; in these instances, I took particular enjoyment in aggressively pursuing the operator in question. The board also had some good employees—particularly Joe Nester and Lisa Ivshin, who now serves as the board's director—with whom I worked to find solutions.

Again, the vast majority of oil companies and contractors were honest and hardworking and provided valuable and safe services. I got along with them very well. I was careful to be fair as well as tough, and in time, some of the bad apples in the industry either cleaned up their act or left the business. Some of that was due to me.

I responded to hundreds of spills, fires, and other emergencies over the years at DEQ and made it a point to treat people with respect and fairness. I believe that this approach is the right way to do things and that it will come back to you when you help people. One time, I responded to a fire near Carey, Mississippi, involving bulk tanks loaded with soybean oil. The tanks had failed in the fire, and a significant amount of soybean oil had spilled, presenting a threat to a nearby creek. The insurance company's arson investigator approached me at the site because he needed to gain access as soon as it was stabilized but was having some difficulty with the local fire department. I helped him out because he had a job to do.

I didn't see this investigator again until nearly two decades later, during the 2010 BP oil spill disaster. By that time, Phil Bryant was no longer investigating arson cases; he was Mississippi's lieutenant governor, and the following year he was elected governor. He remembered that I had helped him and treated him with respect.

My activities at DEQ generated a fair amount of media attention—in print and on local television, from Itawamba County in the north to Jackson County in the south. And all of this reporting focused on my investigations of chemical and oil spills and illegal hazardous waste dumpings rather than on my history as an ex-Klansman invading a foreign country. It appeared that I had finally put my past behind me.

By the end of 1997, I'd been with DEQ for nearly ten years. I was a dedicated and passionate regulator, helping to protect Mississippi's rivers, swamps, and woods, which I'd loved for my entire life. But I was working nights, weekends, and holidays and making only twenty-eight thousand dollars a year. I started thinking about how we would afford college for Forrest and Hillary. Diane had left MEMA to become the training director for the Mississippi Department of Health. She, too, was a state employee with a state salary. To say we were strapped for cash would be an understatement. I didn't see much of a career path into management at DEQ—I was a too politically hot, and the aggressive techniques that had made me such an effective regulator had sometimes rubbed upper management the wrong way. Plus I wanted a new challenge.

Private environmental contractors had previously approached me about a job, and I started paying attention to their offers. Becoming a private contractor would give me more autonomy—and more money. I could continue doing the work I loved as well as support my family. It didn't take long before the right opportunity came along, and my salary doubled overnight to sixty thousand dollars a year.

CHAPTER FOURTEEN

The Big Time

Life as a private contractor was busier and more hectic than it had been working for the state. It was also rewarding, both in environmental and financial terms. I liked to work hard. I liked to make a positive difference—and to run things. This new career eventually led me to a minor role on the world's stage.

I began working as a regional emergency response manager for a company headquartered in Denver. My first major project was working with the EPA to clean up the Hudson Refinery, a Cushing, Oklahoma, facility that had been abandoned for years. We were dealing with some nasty and extremely dangerous chemicals, including anhydrous hydrogen fluoride/hydrofluoric acid and tetraethyl lead. The eight-month project involved many challenges, and I relished overcoming them. Several different companies and industry trade organizations subsequently invited me to give presentations on the unprecedented cleanup operation at the Hudson Refinery and on the techniques I'd developed for dealing with anhydrous hydrogen fluoride.

My new job brought me experience with the other side of the industry and enabled me to develop valuable contacts and long-lasting relationships with chemical and petrochemical companies, railroads, trucking companies, and other contractors in the emergency response business.

One of these relationships was with Barry Thibodeaux, a New Orleans business owner whom I'd previously met when I was with

DEQ. He and I were now competitors on various projects, which allowed me to get to know him better, and I found him to be one of the best business owners—one of the best people—I have ever known. He built his company, United States Environmental Services (USES), by hiring the most capable people he could find and treating them well—like family. His employees reciprocated. In addition to an office in New Orleans, USES had offices in Baton Rouge and Mobile, and when Barry approached me about opening a Jackson office, I jumped at the chance.

I used the contacts I'd developed over the years to grow the new division, hiring the best people I knew from my DEQ and private contractor days—the cream of the crop. Operations manager Robbie Brister, top project manager Don Warren, and I formed a strong and formidable team. Our business model was simple: we treated our employees and their families well and provided a safe and efficient work product to our customers. Integrity, safety, and honesty were first and foremost.

We soon opened another office in Southaven, Mississippi, a suburb of Memphis, and I became the regional manager; and Jason "Jughead" Suggs became the division manager. A short time later, we added an office in Little Rock. With business booming, I became the vice president of emergency response. Any time an incident took place, I traveled to the site. Over time, we continued to grow, opening offices in Nashville, Houston, Birmingham, Biloxi, and Laredo. As my responsibilities and my income increased, I began traveling out of state on hunting and fishing trips. My son, Forrest, and I went pheasant hunting in South Dakota every year. We fished for sturgeon in Oregon and speckled trout and redfish in Venice, Louisiana. I was working harder than ever but was also enjoying my love of the outdoors more than ever.

In a few years I was promoted to chief operating officer, meaning that I was in charge of all USES employees except those in the corporate offices. .

The environmental cleanup industry is a rough-and-tumble, cutthroat business, but I formed solid relationships with a few key competitors, and we traded work back and forth in large spill events. So in a multimillion-dollar emergency like a major oil spill, there might be five or six competitors trying to get a slice of the pie. The relationships I had developed enabled me to capture work for us; in turn, I had great respect for some of our competitors and often brought them in to work with us on large spills. They did the same for us. Good business is all about building positive relationships, and I'm proud of the work I did at USES.

USES had a number of outstanding corporate managers, among them Tom Sumner and Tom Bayham, and we complemented each other to make the whole greater than the sum of the parts. But the most significant part was Barry, who built a company atmosphere of honesty, respect, pride, and caring.

In 2004, Barry and the other two USES owners sold a majority interest in the company to a private equity group, though Barry retained a sizable stake and stayed on as president and CEO. Sumner, Bayham, and I all became minority owners.

In four years, I had gone from managing the Jackson division to owning part of a (much larger) company. Diane and I had spent the first ten years of our marriage living a pretty meager lifestyle. We lived in an old two-bedroom house with peeling paint, a floor furnace for heat, and a couple of window-mounted air conditioners. I spent about eight years and most of what little extra money we had trying to get it into decent shape.

When I went to work for USES, we bought a beautiful home with a backyard swimming pool on forty acres in the country. Part of the acreage was woods, and part was pasture, which I mowed with an air-conditioned tractor. A lake in the front yard was stocked with fish. The property had a two-bedroom guesthouse with its own kitchen and bathroom. I decorated the guesthouse with hunting trophies on the walls and enjoyed hanging out there, sometimes with Forrest.

It sounds idyllic, and it was, but the truth was that I wasn't there that often. I was frequently away working. And when I wasn't working, I was usually hunting or fishing. I had purchased a camp in Grand Isle, Louisiana, bought a boat, and developed a real love for offshore fishing—tuna, amberjack, grouper, mahi-mahi, wahoo, and other big game fish. While I was away working and playing, Diane stayed at home, taking care of our children and taking a job teaching math at the local high school when Forrest and Hillary were older. Our lives had almost completely diverged, and in 2008 we divorced. It was a sad time for all of us. She and I get along very well to this day, and I can say with certainty that Diane is one of the best things that ever happened to me.

On Saturday afternoon, April 24, 2010, I was alone in my yard, planting shrubs and listening to the radio. The big story involved a tornado that had hit Yazoo City, about an hour away from my home in the middle of the state. The news also mentioned BP's Deepwater Horizon oil rig in the Gulf of Mexico, which had exploded four days earlier and had now sunk. It might be leaking oil. The Yazoo tornado sounded like the bigger story: indeed, it killed 10 people and injured nearly 150 others and was the state's worst natural disaster since Hurricane Katrina. But of course, the Deepwater Horizon ultimately turned out to be a far greater catastrophe.

My phone started ringing early that afternoon. We were being mobilized by BP's spill-management company. I began talking to members of my team at USES, subcontractors, and equipment sources for boats and containment booms. We were trying to coordinate our response without knowing how bad it was going to be, not an easy task. I was also talking to my assigned contacts at BP and the disaster response company: I could hear the urgency in their voices.

The Biloxi office became the headquarters for our Mississippi cleanup effort, and I left early the next morning to take charge. The drive took me about three hours, and I spent the entire time on the phone, arranging, coordinating, and mobilizing the forces I thought might be needed to protect the coastline.

Mississippi's Gulf Coast extends from Grand Bay in the east to Pearlington in the west, and in between are marshes, estuaries, beaches, marinas, casinos, restaurants, hotels, and other businesses. Oil or tar balls washing up on the coast would be a financial as well as environmental disaster. I had seen enough birds covered in oil to know what a large spill would do to the region's wildlife. The coastline is partially protected by a string of barrier islands (Petit Bois, Horn, East and West Ship, and Cat), a natural wilderness that is part of Gulf Islands National Seashore and is inhabited by many varieties of birds, mammals, and marine life. A bad enough spill would affect not only the barrier islands but also the area between the coastline and the barrier islands—the Mississippi Sound. But I had little time to think about the potential consequences: I had to focus on preparing to combat the oil that was heading toward my home.

By the time I arrived in Biloxi, the news had gotten worse. The national press had picked up the story, and BP was setting up response-staging locations in Texas, Louisiana, Alabama, and Florida as well as Mississippi and had notified the governors that oil was likely to affect their states.

Mississippi's governor, Haley Barbour, had gone to Yazoo City, his hometown, to assess the tornado damage; as soon as he returned to Jackson, he jumped directly into the BP mess. He called an emergency meeting on April 30 at a National Guard base in Gulfport to discuss and coordinate the Mississippi response. DEQ executive director Trudy Fisher informed me that both Kenny Spriggs, BP's coordinator for Mississippi, and I needed to attend the meeting to brief the governor, his staff, and other state leaders on the response we were organizing. Also in attendance were heads of numerous state agencies, including Fisher, the commissioner of public safety, the adjutant general of the Mississippi National Guard, and the director of the Department of Marine Resources (DMR). Kenny and I were the only nongovernment attendees.

The Coast Guard had set up a conference call with the captain of the Port of New Orleans, Ed Stanton. Ed and I were friends and had worked together for years on various cleanups. When he found out that I was on the call, he directed many of the questions to me, the only oil spill expert in the room. My responses answered many of Governor Barbour's questions, too, and over the next few years, he and I formed a solid relationship as we formulated not only the initial response but also a long-term strategy for remediation of the barrier islands.

When the meeting ended, Governor Barbour said he wanted to see the spill up close. He ordered the National Guard to provide us with a Blackhawk helicopter so he could fly over and see any approaching oil for himself, and he directed me to come along. We didn't fly all the way to the Macondo blowout, where the Deepwater Horizon rig had sunk, but we did make a close inspection of the Mississippi coastline and barrier islands. We couldn't see much—yet. When we returned to the base, the press was swarming, and the governor again instructed me to come along to help answer questions. I'd been questioned by the press before, of course, but this was the first time I'd been in front of the national media. By the end of the conference, I had become the go-to guy for Mississippi's response to the disaster. The next day, a photograph of Governor Barbour and me talking appeared on the front page of Mississippi's largest newspaper, the *Jackson Clarion-Ledger*.

For the first few weeks of the spill, BP had me attend public meetings to explain our response operations. I faced hostile crowds and angry elected officials as I gave details about the defensive measures we were implementing. These meetings were very unpleasant—I was serving as the public face of a company that was threatening these communities. One of my meetings was in Gulfport, and one man there was particularly aggressive. He repeatedly stood and interrupted me, calling me a liar or making other accusations against BP. A few days later, BP sent me to attend a meeting held by the Harrison County Board of Supervisors. Board chair Connie Rockco did a good job of keeping order, although the members of the crowd were upset and aggressive. About halfway through the meeting, I was speaking about the deployment of boom to protect harbors and sensitive areas when I was interrupted by the same man who had been at the Gulfport meeting. He again called me a liar and made even more disparaging remarks. When the meeting ended, I asked Connie who the son of a bitch was. He was Leo "Chipper" McDermott, mayor of Pass Christian. She gave me his cell phone number, and I called him later that day. I explained who I was and said, "I know you're upset with the spill, and I can't blame you one damn bit. I'd like to come meet with you and explain what we're doing and personally address any problems you may have."

We met at 7:30 the next morning in the parking lot at the Pass Christian Small Craft Harbor. He escorted me to a large sport fisherman yacht, where a few local fishermen were waiting. They all opened beers, and someone handed one to me. Now, I don't mind partaking in a cold beer, but I'm not one to drink in the morning, and I damn sure didn't need to be drinking with all of the issues I was dealing with that day. But I was willing to do whatever it took to get Chipper off my ass. Chipper wasn't drinking, but I began talking with them and sipping. When my beer was just over half empty, Chipper popped the top on another and handed it to me. This went on for about two hours, and then we shook hands. Chipper thanked me for meeting with them, and he became one of my biggest allies on the coast—and a good friend. He's still the mayor, and I always stop by and visit with him when I'm in the area.

The way I dealt with Chipper is characteristic of how I deal with problems—head-on and aggressively. I am not one to shy away from a problem or avoid it: I look it in the eye and do my best to solve it.

Between April and August 2010, I worked at least sixteen hours a day, seven days a week. And for the following six months, I was still putting in around twelve hours a day, six days a week. My phone usually started ringing at six o'clock in the morning and didn't stop until ten at night. If I was in a meeting or on another call for an hour, my voicemail filled up. I had no personal life at all. My life was nothing but meetings, travel, decisions and more decisions, and problems and more problems. And at stake were hundreds of millions of dollars and the livelihoods of thousands of people and the lives of millions of animals—the ecological health of an entire region.

The Deepwater Horizon disaster was a big deal, dominating the news for months. My role in BP's overall response was minor, but I was quite prominent in the Mississippi cleanup. I am a very competitive person and set a goal from the outset for USES to be the prime contractor on the Mississippi cleanup, with virtually all subcontractors reporting to us. As a result of the relationships I'd developed over the previous twenty years, I was in a good position to capture a large portion of the work to be done in our state.

I spent May 2010 implementing oil spill defensive operations across the Mississippi coast. At the same time, Forrest was finishing his first semester of college at Ole Miss, where he had enrolled in January. When his grades came out, it was obvious he'd had a really good time but had not applied himself academically. Every parent would love to see their child make a 4.0 GPA: Forrest's GPA had a 4 and an 0 in it, but in the reverse order. I'd learned what hard work was all about at a young age and thought it time that Forrest learn the same thing, so I put him to work on the oil spill. He brought about a dozen of his college buddies down with him, and they spent the summer working out of our Bayou Caddy forward-response office in Hancock County, deploying boom and performing oil cleanup operations. When the fall semester rolled around, all but four of them went back to college. Forrest, Brad Taggart, Land Smathers, and Clay Horton stayed on the cleanup and performed admirably. I had wanted Forrest to gain an appreciation for the value of education, so over the next year, he worked on Ship and Cat Islands, picking up tar balls.

At that point, he was eager to go back to college. He enrolled at Mississippi College and became an excellent student, graduating in 2015 with a degree in Accounting. He got a job at the Mississippi Department of Revenue and enrolled in the MBA program at Millsaps College. Sometimes a dose of reality, coupled with hard labor, can be a valuable learning experience. It certainly worked for us.

The competition for spill-cleanup work was fierce. Enormous amounts of money were involved, and the economy was in a recession. Some of the contractors with whom I was competing were big political heavyweights willing to do nearly anything for a piece of the action. I remained focused, however, and outmaneuvered my competitors. Leadership is just as much about being willing to compromise as it is about taking a firm stance, and I used both approaches. By late June 2010, I'd captured almost all of the work in Hancock and Harrison Counties and subcontracted it to various businesses, nearly all of them Mississippi-based.

One company with whom I compromised was Yates Construction, Mississippi's largest construction company, with almost ten thousand employees. Bill Yates is a brilliant businessman and a great strategic thinker, and he and his company used their connections to make the case to high-ranking BP officials that Yates should be a prime contractor. I was spending more and more of my time trying to keep them at bay, so finally I elected to bring them under my tent. Bill and I met at Mugshots restaurant in Flowood and cut a deal to hire them as a subcontractor to perform cleanup operations on Cat Island.

Governor Barbour centralized Mississippi's response to the BP oil spill, an approach that differed significantly from that used next door in Louisiana, where responses were controlled by the parishes. Because the State of Mississippi was coordinating the cleanup, I was able to make a big difference. , I began developing close relationships with local elected officials across the coast. I met every day with mayors, county supervisors, state senators and representatives, and other elected leaders. All of them wanted things—say, five hundred feet of boom to protect the entrance to a small craft harbor. The only way to get that allocation was to go through the twisty channels of approval at Unified Command, an umbrella organization established to link together all the different stakeholders, including BP, the Gulf states, and federal government entities (e.g., the US Coast Guard and the EPA as well as many others). Unified

Command was a bureaucratic nightmare, and the people there were focused on the big problems and not inclined to pay attention to such small things as five hundred feet of boom. In contrast, I made it my business to help the local officials, getting them the boom or whatever resources they needed (without Unified Command being aware of what was happening, of course).

When local politicians referred constituents who needed jobs, I hired or helped hire these people—I don't know exactly how many, but it had to have been close to a hundred. The local politicians supported their constituents, and I supported them. Everyone wins. I was effective because I paid attention not only to the big picture but also to the hundreds or maybe thousands of little pictures.

The scope of the disaster mushroomed as time went on. BP needed more resources than USES alone—or any company—had. We needed more work boats, with experienced crews to handle them, more containment boom, and of course more people—thousands of people. BP had to reach out to other companies from all over the country.

One of my major concerns was making sure we had equipment and people in place when the oil hit the beaches. We needed more than just oil-spill contractors: we needed construction companies, earthmoving operations, electrical contractors, plumbing contractors, and a variety of others that could provide people, equipment, and solid management skills. I sought to build a coalition of the best of these companies and to do it before the oil hit. They had resources and equipment we lacked, and we could train them how to clean up oil.

Both BP and I faced tremendous pressure to use Mississippi companies rather than out-of-state contractors. Lieutenant Governor Phil Bryant told me, "George, I will support you as long as you put Mississippi companies and Mississippi workers first. Mississippi first, Mississippi first." Governor Barbour pointed out that two Mississippi companies, T. L. Wallace Construction and Eutaw Construction, had done excellent work in the wake of Katrina, but he didn't push me to use them. That attitude also was characteristic of Governor Barbour's staff. During the early days of the spill, before the oil hit the coast, I spoke with chief of staff Paul Hurst because I was hearing from politically influential people who were eager to get work on the cleanup so that they could begin making money. Hurst told me, "This is not about politics. This is about protecting the state and doing what's right. You can send them to me and I'll deal with them." Decisions were most often based on good policy and doing what was right, with politics wielding little influence.

Wallace Construction and Eutaw Construction had good reputations, so I reached out to them and to dozens of others, including ones on the coast. It was important to give work to the coastal companies because they and other residents of the region were going to be hardest hit by the economic impact of the spill. I spent a solid month building the coalition, which was strong both operationally and politically. We were prepared to mobilize, manage, and support thousands of workers when the time came.

The BP leaders assigned to Mississippi were not perfect, but they faced an unprecedented and almost impossible task—responding to an enormous spill over nearly seventeen hundred miles of coastline from Galveston Bay in Texas to the Florida Keys. BP deserves credit for taking responsibility for the cleanup and for assigning Maureen Johnson, the company's vice president of operations technology for the Western Hemisphere, to serve as the company's liaison in Mississippi. Mo (as everyone calls her) did an amazing job of navigating the minefield of our state and local officials.

When I first met Mo, I didn't much care for her, and I don't think she was particularly fond of me. She was an engineer, with a dry and direct no-nonsense personality. But as I watched her deal with furious mayors and county officials as well as almost every state-level official, I came to trust and respect her. And she came to understand that I was working hard, keeping in mind with the interests not just of Mississippi but also of BP. She didn't care about rank and status, she told the honest truth, no sugarcoating. If she said, "No, we can't do that," she meant it. But if she said she was going to do something, she would follow through, no matter the cost to BP or anyone else. Not long after the blowout was plugged on July 15, Mo went back to her normal duties. At this point Heidi Grether became my primary point of contact with BP: like Mo, Heidi performed one hell of a job under very difficult and trying circumstances. In July 2016, Heidi was appointed as the executive director of the Michigan Department of Environmental Quality, where she inherited the Flint water crisis. When I heard of Heidi's appointment, I thought, "Well, the Flint crisis will be junior league to Heidi after the political storms she weathered during the Mississippi BP response."

Mo and Heidi worked particularly well with Governor Barbour's two staffers in charge of the spill, Patrick Sullivan and Ashley Edwards, and the three of them fought and won some major battles on Mississippi's behalf. I was lucky enough to become a part of that team, which enabled me to really get things done. Other members of BP's talented and dedicated team on the ground included Lisa Houghton, Dawn Bobbitt, J. P. Presley, Marti Powers and Pat Presley, among many others.

Governor Barbour and his staffers, too, developed trust in me and my opinions. I often heard from his office when they were preparing to make decisions, and I sat in on many meetings and conference calls with officials from the state government and from BP. Governor Barbour made sure I knew he had my back, telling me, "I want you to be aggressive and take risks." So I was and did.

One Sunday morning in June 2010, I got a very early morning phone call from one of DMR's marine patrol boats. We had placed thousands of feet of containment boom across Biloxi Bay between Deer Island and Ocean Springs. In the middle we had left a gate, approximately five hundred feet wide, that could be opened and closed to allow boat and barge traffic to move in and out when no oil was present. A USES vessel remained on guard at the gate 24/7, ready to close it if oil appeared.

The DMR patrol boat had observed a ten-acre area of water covered with large tar patties and tar balls that were nearing the gate. But closing the gate required US Coast Guard approval, since we would be shutting down a major navigable waterway. The DMR patrol boat wanted me to direct the USES boat to close the gate immediately to prevent the oil from entering.

The threat was imminent. The Coast Guard bureaucracy might take a long time on a Sunday morning. Was I willing to take responsibility for closing a navigable waterway without official approval? I remembered Governor Barbour's words and decided that yes, I was. I called our boat and directed that the gate immediately be closed, and then I dispatched Mississippi's only skimmer, which was deployed at Biloxi Bay, to begin recovering the oil. By the end of the day, all of the patties and tar balls had been recovered. No oil got past our containment boom.

Sure enough, the next day, the wrath of the Coast Guard came down: I had no authority to close the gate and dispatch a skimmer. BP officials at Unified Command had been chastised for my actions, and they let me know how they felt about it. But real leadership is sometimes about doing what's right, not necessarily about what is considered acceptable or politically correct. I was comfortable with my decision.

I grew to admire Governor Barbour's leadership skills, particularly as I saw them on display during the weekly conference calls involving BP officials and the governors of the affected states. Barbour's style was to take charge and to collaborate with BP leaders, among them CEO Tony Hayward and chief operating officer Doug Suttles. Barbour picked his battles, and when he lost, he moved on to the next one. And he came up with creative solutions. For example, Unified Command deployed only a single oil-skimming boat to Mississippi: almost all of the skimmers were sent to south Louisiana, which was where the bulk of the oil was. But Mississippi also needed them. We were under tremendous pressure to skim the oil before it hit Mississippi beaches. At most every press conference and public meeting the question arose "Where are the skimmers?"

Barbour's solution was to build our own and use BP money to pay for them. With the company's permission, we arranged to have ten skimmers built for Mississippi alone, and they came off the production line in mid-July, about the time the Macondo well was plugged. They ultimately were not needed, which led some in the media to charge that the skimmers were a waste of money or a boondoggle for the companies that built them. But such accusations are merely an example of hindsight being 20/20. If more oil had leaked and the spill had reached the Mississippi coastline, those skimmers would have prevented a deluge of tar balls.

Governor Barbour also got BP to pay for twenty million dollars' worth of barrier fencing to keep oil from getting into Mississippi's estuaries and other environmentally sensitive areas. Local officials had been demanding extra protection and getting nowhere, but Barbour stepped in, and then the mayors and county supervisors worked with DMR to decide where the fencing should be placed.

Governor Barbour was an effective politician because he understood that his role was to be a consensus builder. But make no mistake—in instances where he failed to build a consensus but thought he was right, he didn't hesitate to make a decision and move forward. Being an integral part of this process was rewarding and exhausting. The Deepwater Horizon response consumed my life and challenged me at every turn.

About two months into the response, I was summoned to the DMR for a meeting with Barbour and BP CEO Hayward. When I arrived, I saw the governor's wife, Marsha Barbour, sitting outside the building in the sunshine. She asked me to join her to talk about oil-spill cleanup—different technologies, what would work and what wouldn't. She had done tremendous work on the Mississippi Gulf Coast after Katrina and wanted to help after the BP disaster, too. I thought of the governor and the CEO waiting for me upstairs, but suddenly I'd had enough. I'd been working nonstop, spending hours and hours on phone calls, meetings, decisions, arguments, and problems. I needed a break. So I sat down on the bench, silenced my phone, and chatted with Marsha for about an hour.

We were still there when her husband, Hayward, and their entourages came out and saw us on the bench. They came up to us, and I said, "I'm sorry for standing y'all up, Governor. I've been enjoying a very pleasant conversation with Mrs. Barbour."

I think Hayward understood. Like me, he wanted his life back, if even for just a little while.

CHAPTER FIFTEEN

Swimming with the Sharks

Newspaper and magazine articles, TV newscasts, and websites and blogs have all reported on the whole Deepwater Horizon mess. They've whispered and shouted about backroom deals, unscrupulous and/or shady operators, political payoffs, influence peddling, and all kinds of other nefarious stuff. I'm sure some of these things are true, at least partially, but from what I've seen, these aspects have been grossly magnified.

I can't speak for other states, the Mississippi response to the BP spill is a positive story. There were no smoke-filled rooms where deals were cut for political reasons, and I would know: I was the gatekeeper to the hundreds of millions of BP dollars for response work, and I had the authority to decide who got what if any work. Not once was I told to give work to any contractor or pressured in any way by an elected official. But as former governor Haley Barbour likes to say, "The press doesn't report on planes that land safely," so I doubt we'll ever see an in-depth story on the inside workings of the Mississippi BP response. It definitely wasn't flawless, and it unquestionably had problems, but it wasn't fraught with political payoffs, kickbacks, or other forms of corruption.

With so much money swirling around and the inherently unsettled nature of disasters, it's no wonder that the rumor mill and emotions ran high. It's natural to be emotional if one of the biggest man-made disasters in history happens in your own backyard, jeopardizing your home, your livelihood, your family's future, and the beauty of the land on which you live. It's natural to be angry, to want to blame someone and make them pay.

It's also natural to try to turn the disaster to your advantage. The Deepwater Horizon disaster represented a huge economic opportunity not only for good and honest companies but also for shady operators who just wanted to make a quick buck. Telling them apart wasn't always easy.

Some contractors who wanted a piece of the oil-spill-recovery business weren't happy with their share and blamed me, making their feelings known via anonymous comments on Internet sites such as the *Biloxi Sun Herald*, *Slabbed*, and *Jackson Jambalaya*. When I eventually found out who was behind those comments, it turned out to be either people to whom I had refused to give work or people who I had removed from the cleanup effort for unethical behavior. In short, it was sour grapes.

In several instances, potential subcontractors either explicitly or implicitly offered me financial rewards if I gave them work. I had zero tolerance for these unscrupulous contractors and vendors. On one occasion, during introductions for a meeting about barges needed to stage our response on the barrier islands, a company owner slipped me a folded piece of paper as we shook hands. I didn't look at it immediately, but when I opened the note later, it said, *I will give you one percent of all billings*. And he'd actually signed his name. We badly needed his barges, and I would have leased them, but I didn't want to do business with people who would offer kickbacks. I got the barges from someone else.

The only other time I was blatantly offered a kickback or bribe involved a subcontractor who was already working for USES but wasn't getting the volume of work he desired. He was just plain greedy. After he set up a meeting and asked me to use more of his resources, he said, "We want you to be a part of this with us. I want you to share in this with us. I have a private jet that can fly you on weekend getaways if you want." I politely declined his offer. A few days later, one of my BP contacts, Pat Presley, informed me that this subcontractor had been sending emails to BP officials about getting more of his assets working and copying various elected officials on his emails—an obvious and foolish attempt to intimidate the company. This was the final straw. I was done with this unscrupulous character and informed Pat that I intended to remove this contractor from the response. Pat had no objections, so over the next several months, I weeded out their assets and we moved on without them.

Even prior to the Deepwater Horizon incident, the spill cleanup business was ferociously competitive and sometimes cutthroat. Nevertheless, I had forged strong alliances with several major competitors. It had only taken me a few months to push our competition out of Harrison and Hancock Counties, but Jackson County was split between USES and Clean Harbors, based out of Boston. Though I was friendly with Virgil Blanchard, who managed Clean Harbors, the company was large and publicly traded, and I worried that its executives or shareholders might decide to come after our work in Harrison and Hancock Counties.

Figuring that a good offense is the best defense, I made the strategic decision to go after the Jackson County work and push Clean Harbors out. I knew that this would be difficult: Blanchard was a seasoned and capable oil spill professional, and his company was doing a good job. But they had an Achilles heel: they did not have an office in Mississippi. Governor Barbour and Lieutenant Governor Bryant had made it abundantly clear that they wanted Mississippi companies performing the Mississippi cleanup operations. Though the USES headquarters was in New Orleans, we had three offices in Mississippi and a long history of hiring Mississippi workers and spending tens of millions of dollars with Mississippi vendors.

On a cool and dreary Sunday morning in November 2010, I decided to make my move. I had solidified USES in Harrison and Hancock Counties, and we were doing an outstanding job. By this time, almost all of the work being performed was on the barrier islands, which had taken the brunt of the oil. Horn and Petit Bois Islands in Jackson County had been particularly heavily affected.

My coalition was made up of dozens of Mississippi-based companies working under two prime USES subcontractors, Yates Construction and a joint venture between T. L. Wallace Construction and Eutaw Construction. Yates and Wallace-Eutaw had been jockeying back and forth, each hoping to get a bigger piece of the pie. Refereeing among these three powerhouses was a never-ending task—I privately referred to the owners of the three companies as "the alpha males" because they were not accustomed to being subcontractors. We were working on cleaning up Cat and East and West Ship Islands, but Horn was the grand prize, with hundreds of Clean Harbors laborers out there every day, weather permitting. If my plan succeeded, not only would USES capture all of the Mississippi work, but my problems with turf battles among the three powerful subcontractors would be solved.

On that dreary November morning in my rental house in Pass Christian, I decided I'd been patient long enough and it was time to move. I rarely called Governor Barbour on his cell phone out of respect for his hectic schedule, so I sent Marsha a text and asked her to have him call me. When he did, I explained my plan: I would split the work up by county. Yates would get all of Jackson County, and Wallace-Eutaw would get all of Harrison and Hancock. This relatively equitable split of the work would please all three parties. I pointed out to the governor that the Jackson County work was being performed by a Boston company with no presence in our state before the spill. Although Clean Harbors had never invested in Mississippi or hired Mississippians prior to the disaster, they did have several Mississippi companies working as subcontractors. I told Barbour that I would ask Yates to subcontract the Mississippi companies working for Clean Harbors. And if he would sell my plan to BP, we would have an all-Mississippi response involving dozens of Mississippi subcontractors. That was all Governor Barbour needed to hear. He went to work persuading BP.

The idea took a while to work its way through the channels, but BP ultimately approved it. USES was awarded virtually all of the

Mississippi work and took over Jackson County operations. Strategic thinking, compromise, and patience had finally paid off. I was now in charge of all operations being performed in the state.

I was riding high on a wave of professional successes, but my personal life was more complicated. A few years earlier, my mother had been diagnosed with dementia, and my father, who was suffering from macular degeneration, had cared for her as long as he could but was finally forced to place her into a treatment center. When Dad was no longer able to live alone, he moved in with my sister, Lucienne, in Biloxi.

Visiting Mom was heartbreaking for all of us. She no longer had no idea who we were or even who *she* was. One day in 2011, I visited her in the nursing home on the coast where she was being cared for and was shocked at her condition. She was skin and bones, lying on her side in the bed and curled up in the fetal position, and nearly unconscious. I talked to her and touched her but received no response or reaction of any kind. Nothing. Her nurse said that had become her "norm." I stayed only a short time; although she was still medically alive, I realized that my mom was gone—what remained was only a shell of the wonderful person she had been. She clung to life for another eight months before passing away at age eighty-four. It was actually a relief when she died.

I left the nursing home that day and drove down Highway 90 along the beach, trying to clear my mind, and stopped at Ken Combs Pier in Gulfport. Several people were fishing on the pier, and I remembered how when I was a child, Mom took me fishing and crabbing at Fort Morgan near Gulf Shores, Alabama. It seemed like yesterday.

It was a sad time, but I had to get back to work. Not only was my phone constantly was ringing with issues related to the spill cleanup, but a scandal was brewing.

I had been coordinating the BP response with DMR for a couple of years, so my name was often associated closely with that department, and the state had given me an office in the same building that housed the DMR and most of the other state agencies. My office was sandwiched between the offices occupied by Patrick Sullivan, who was one of Governor Barbour's main staffers, and the DMR's executive director, Dr. Bill Walker. In 2012, the *Biloxi Sun Herald* began digging into rumors that Walker was involved in some shenanigans.

In May 2010, Dr. Walker's son, Scott, a lobbyist, started bringing in companies he represented to try to get them hired to perform services on the spill. Scott took them to meet his father and then to meet me in the office next door. Sometimes Dr. Walker and I met jointly with Scott and his clients.

Dr. Walker couldn't hire anyone since the response was funded primarily by the private sector, and he had no authority to dictate who I could hire. But I soon began to feel uneasy about what was going on. Dr. Walker never directly asked me to hire any of Scott's clients, but I had concerns that if I didn't, I might damage my working relationship with the DMR, and I needed to be on good terms with the agency—and with Dr. Walker—if I was going to do my job effectively.

A few days after the first time Scott came by with a client, Patrick Sullivan came into my office and closed the door behind him. I could tell that something was troubling him. I had met with him dozens of times before, and he'd never closed the door. He told me that the governor's office wasn't going to tell me who to hire or not hire, but they didn't like it that Scott was bringing clients in to meet with his father and me. "You don't have to hire any of those people," he said. "If they offer a good service to protect the coast or do some cleanup, fine. But the way they're going about it is pushing the envelope too far." The message was clear: I should be very cautious about hiring anyone represented by Scott Walker.

I followed up with another of the governor's staffers, Ashley Edwards, who not only echoed Patrick's concerns but was even more vocal about not using clients represented by Scott. But I still didn't want to alienate Dr. Walker. So in spite of the numerous demands on my time, I continued to meet with Scott's clients, listened to their pitches, went out to dinner with them, and gave them special attention. With only one exception—a coast-based company that was well qualified to perform the services and that did a good a job for us—I did not hire his clients. Ironically, at least two companies would have gotten work from me had they not been represented by Scott. Over the course of the spill response, USES hired 143 subcontractors and vendors to work on the Mississippi response: only 1 was represented by Scott.

In 2013, the FBI started investigating whether Dr. Walker and the DMR had misspent the state's money. The FBI agent leading the investigation was Matt Campbell, and I started hearing his name when people called to tell me that he was asking questions about my relationship with Dr. Walker. I wasn't surprised—I had been seen publicly at many events with Dr. Walker and Scott, and I'd handled hundreds of millions of dollars flowing through USES, which is a ripe environment for kickbacks. But I also wasn't worried—I never came close to doing anything shady.

Campbell eventually spoke with me directly, and the first thing he said was, "You're not suspected of any wrongdoing." He'd spent months digging into financial records, emails, and bank accounts and talking to dozens of elected officials, contractors, vendors, and businesspeople. He told me no one had had anything bad to say about me, and he'd already determined that hiring Scott as a lobbyist was a surefire way not to get any business from me.

The FBI agent was an aggressive guy, not afraid to step on toes, no matter whose they were, and not delicate about it, either. I thought of him as the Eliot Ness of white-collar crime for south Mississippi. He wasn't going to rest until he got his man. And he did. Bill and Scott Walker pled guilty to several federal felonies in 2014 and were sentenced to prison terms.

One day in 2013, I was having lunch with Mississippi's attorney general, Jim Hood, and he said, "I was watching all that was going on and what you were involved in during BP, and I was worried about you. You were swimming with the sharks. I don't know how you managed not to get bit." My answer: "I never put myself in a position that would give one of the sharks an opportunity to bite me."

The spill made me a public figure. I routinely attended and spoke at meetings with high-ranking elected officials, including the governor, lieutenant governor, secretary of state, and state agency heads; US and Mississippi senators and representatives; mayors and county supervisors; and business leaders from across the region. The Mississippi Senate's Oil Spill Oversight Committee called me in several times to answer questions.

In early June 2010, I received a phone call from a number I didn't recognize. I answered anyway. The caller was Anita Lee, an investigative reporter with the *Biloxi Sun Herald* who I did not know. US congressman Gene Taylor had toured a BP staging area, and I'd escorted him. After the *Sun Herald* ran a front-page picture of Taylor and me, someone made an anonymous online comment that mentioned my background as a Klansman and mercenary. Anita's interest had been piqued, and she told me that the paper was going to do a story on what she called my "colorful past." Would I be willing to talk with her?

I was concerned that a story about my days in the Klan and my time in prison would hinder what I was trying to accomplish in the Gulf, and I told Anita my thoughts. She said that the paper was going to do the story with or without my cooperation, so I said, "Well, if you're going to do it, you need to hear my side of the story. I don't have anything to hide."

Anita and I spoke in person for about an hour and a half and then did a couple of follow-up phone interviews. When the article was finished, she gave me two days' notice before it appeared. I met with BP officials as well as with the governor's staff, the management of the DEQ and the DMR, and various elected officials. I told them all about my past, warts and all. I also told them that I'd been very young and that those activities it did not reflect who I was now.

The front-page story appeared in the *Sun Herald* on June 16, 2010: "Reformed Klansman Plays Leading Role in Gulf Cleanup."

It featured a photo of me talking to US congressman Gene Taylor. Anita had asked tough questions about my racial views and the KKK, but her story was fair. That was all I wanted. The story was syndicated by the McClatchy news service and appeared in various newspapers and on websites, including the *Huffington Post*. I waited for the storm to hit.

To my surprise, there wasn't one. I never heard a single negative comment from anyone. Instead, I received text messages and phone calls from many state and local elected officials who congratulated me on the positive changes I'd made in my life. The support came from across the political spectrum, all the way from Mississippi's Republican governor and lieutenant governor to Connie Moran, the liberal and progressive Democratic mayor of Ocean Springs. Most of the people at BP basically shrugged, seeming to view it as a nonstory.

However, the story did cause a lot of people to ask me, "How did you go from *that* to where you are now?" "You wouldn't believe it if I told you," became my standard reply.

That's when I first began entertaining the idea of writing a book. *Why not tell them?* But then I would squash the idea. *Why delve so deeply into controversial and painful subjects?* I argued with myself: *My God George, you're a high school dropout, an ex-Kluxer, and an ex-con. Come to your senses! Don't go there!* Ultimately, my responsibilities with the oil spill pushed the idea aside for the time being.

In 2012, USES completed the last of our BP-cleanup operations, and I returned to a more normal routine. But I had changed a lot since April 2010. I was burned out and lacked the energy to return to managing a company that employed more than a thousand men and women, so I gave up the title of chief operating officer as well as most of my duties and became executive vice president, with minimal day-to-day responsibilities.

I was working from my home out in the country, and for the first time in a long while, I had some free time. I began thinking again about writing a book and returned to my old internal arguments about whether it was a good idea. I was in no rush to make a decision of such magnitude.

While I was ruminating, USES held a Jackson retreat for the company's senior managers as well as several investment bankers and private equity executives. The final night featured a wild-game dinner for the attendees, and I was the host. The main courses were grilled elk steaks, venison sausage, and venison roast—pretty standard for one of my dinners. I got a little creative with the appetizers, though: a delicious gumbo made from two water moccasins and a rat snake as well as small pieces of frog legs. I also served grilled nutria, coon, and armadillo.

The guests arrived and began drinking fine whiskey, wine, and ice-cold beer. After they were nice and relaxed, I announced the wild-game dinner would be followed by a team-building exercise involving clues to figure out what they'd just eaten. Although some were nervous, all were good sports and played along. Though they loved the food and raved about how delicious it was, almost everyone was shocked to learn what they'd actually eaten (especially because I told them that the frog legs were coon testicles), and a few people became physically ill and/or a bit angry. But most took it well.

In 2014, an icon of the oil-spill-cleanup industry, Sammy Jones, was diagnosed with terminal cancer, and another industry giant, Ben Benson, began organizing an event to honor Sammy. Held in Slidell, Louisiana, the gathering attracted the who's who among oil spill contractors. The event featured a fund-raiser for Sammy's family that included a live auction of five donated Yeti coolers. Harry Marsh, Virgil Blanchard, Nelson Fetgatter, Brook Guidry, and I each purchased a cooler for three thousand dollars and then donated them back so that they could be auctioned again, raising several thousand more. We had all been fierce competitors over the years and had battled one another for a seat at the table of the major oil spills, but we came together to help one of our own when it was most needed.

I continued to host wild-game dinners and other functions at my home and to contemplate whether to write an autobiography. When I finally decided to go ahead and tell my story. I had a lot of free time on my hands and I needed a new challenge. I'd come so far and experienced so much. I had kept the promise I made to myself in that Tallahassee prison cell. It was time to answer that question: *How did I get from there to here?*

CHAPTER SIXTEEN

No Blinding Lights

I am at best skeptical when people claim suddenly to "see the light." I saw a few of these "conversions" when I was in prison, and I always thought that these people were just trying on a con—seeking an early release or a justification for ratting on someone else. Real internal change doesn't happen in a flash. Events can trigger a process of evolution, but this process takes time.

I didn't wake up one morning suddenly having changed from being a card-carrying Klansman, mercenary, and felon. I have evolved over the years—sometimes consciously, sometimes subconsciously; sometimes deliberately, sometimes by accident. I am much different from the person I was thirty years ago. I'm different from the person I was five years ago. And I'm still evolving—I'll be different five years from now, too.

I grew up in a segregated world and didn't question the social mores of that time. In my teens and early twenties, I had no patience with anyone who disagreed with me. I made no room for them in my life; in fact, I didn't think they needed to be on the earth at all. I was intolerant of those who disagreed with me on politics, race relations, or just about any other issue.

Prison jump-started my evolution. At times, it was brutal and vicious. I saw heads beaten in, savage fights, filth, and despair. I lived with the worst of society, men who had committed horrific crimes, But some of them became my friends. And that's where I decided to start down the path to becoming a better person. I wouldn't go back and change my experiences for anything. It's part of me now.

Writing letters for Leon brought me the first flickering of light—not a blinding floodlight that changed me immediately, but a little candle that dimmed now and then over the years but never went out completely once it had been lit. In prison, I started to question myself and my beliefs. I considered that I might have been wrong. I was lucky, because I saw that prison made most people worse, not better. Their racial beliefs grew more extreme, not less. They became more violent, not less. Rehabilitation was rare. Again, I have Leon to thank for the fact that I defied the odds. I have no idea what became of Leon, but I suspect it wasn't good. That's a shame.

After college, I met, worked with, and became friends with people who were very different from me. I could talk to and laugh with these friends, and I invited them to my home. More than just my racist viewpoint evolved. I wanted to become an educated person, to be a good father, to live with integrity and decency. I am still walking that road.

I'm a political conservative on most issues, but I'm liberal on others. I typically detest the extremes on either side. The events of my life taught me the value of compromise and how to listen respectfully to the viewpoints of others. We must all work together to find and build on common ground if we want to progress. This is true leadership—the only kind that works. I try to put these beliefs into action.

When Governor Barbour left office in January 2012, he pardoned a number of felons, a controversial move that received a lot of negative press. Haley and Marsha Barbour asked me to assist one of the pardoned men, Anthony McCray, in finding employment. A black man who'd been imprisoned for murder, Anthony had become a trusty at the Governor's Mansion. When I met him, he reminded me of Leon. The two men were similar in stature, had very dark skin, and were soft-spoken. While interviewing Anthony, I felt a strange connection to Leon, and I wanted to give Anthony a second chance—a chance I doubt that Leon ever got. I hired Anthony at USES because I believe in second chances. I was given second chances when I got out of prison.

Anthony turned out to be one of the best hires I ever made. He was a stellar employee with an excellent work ethic and a good person. And more important, he turned out to be a friend. Anthony no longer works at USES, but we still keep in touch on a weekly basis.

I, too, left USES, starting my own company, Malvaney and Associates, in 2014. I'm proud of the job I did with USES and probably would have remained there, but success had changed the company, and I didn't fit in with those changes.

In 2010, Barry Thibodeaux had wanted to step back from the company, and his majority partner, a private equity firm, brought in a new company president. For the next year or so, the management style didn't change much, mainly because BP kept us too busy, but in 2011, the changes began in earnest.

USES had been family oriented, putting employees first. Under the new management, however, maximizing profits became paramount. I didn't like what I saw happening, and when the equity firm sold out to another firm in 2014, things got even worse. As chief operating officer, I'd worked hard to make USES profitable, but I didn't like what I saw after Barry Thibodeaux stepped back from running the company. The new managers weren't bad people, but they suffered from extreme corporate greed and simply didn't understand human beings, motivations, and relationships. And they focused so intently on maximizing profits, squeezing every dime they could out of the company, that they were oblivious to the damage they were doing. In just a few years, they practically destroyed USES.

At Malvaney and Associates, I use my relationships and my skill in building consensus to help other companies. I act as a liaison between private firms and government, helping them to find compromises that both parties can live with.

In July 2017, my lifelong quest to avoid boredom and find adventure and new challenges caught up with me again. I became an owner of a relatively new environmental contracting firm, Enhanced Environmental and Emergency Services (E3). Our corporate office in Clinton, Mississippi, performs chemical/oil spill emergency response and industrial cleaning operations, and we have six offices servicing the southern United States. My business partner, Tim Parkman, and I have adopted a simple but highly successful business model: take good care of and value your employees, and provide your clients with a safe and efficient work product.

I enjoy my work, which continues to challenge me and offer me plenty of opportunities to improve the environment of my beloved Mississippi. And I continue to feed my lifelong love of nature. My home is located on several hundred acres of mature hardwood timber, complete with lakes and streams. I have a cabin on the water where I relax (and where I've worked on this book). My son, Forrest, lives in another small cabin located above the lake and enjoys hunting and fishing; my daughter, Hillary, enjoys target shooting and sometimes brings along my grandson, Patrick, who was born on December 8, 2015. I fondly recall teaching Forrest about nature, hunting, and fishing. And although Patrick is still just a toddler, I'm looking forward to teaching him the same things.

My favorite causes span the political spectrum. I am an ardent supporter both of the Second Amendment and of environmental causes such as antiwhaling activists. I admire the efforts of Captain Paul Watson and the Sea Shepherds, a nonprofit organization that attempts to disrupt Japanese whaling expeditions. I don't always agree with his tactics, but I, too, want whales and sea lions to survive for future generations.

Outside of work, I spend time helping homeless pets. Shelters are full of cats and dogs, who are restricted to small cages and spend very little time outside. I donate my money and time to local no-kill shelters, pay vet bills for rescue operations, and adopt rescue dogs myself. My favorite organizations are Community Animal Rescue and Adoption (CARA), Animal Rescue Fund (ARF), and Cheshire Abbey, all of which are located in Jackson and perform outstanding services.

I am also active in Big House Books, a small nonprofit that provides books to convicts in Mississippi prisons. I learned about the group when I saw their booth at the 2016 Mississippi Book Festival. A volunteer opened a three-ring binder that contained letters from convicts and urged me to read a few of them so that I could understand what they were experiencing. I didn't need to read the letters: I already knew exactly what they said. I had been there. I dropped a hundred-dollar bill in the collection jar. And I continue to provide financial support for this fine organization.

I still hunt and fish, but I'm not the avid hunter I once was. I still love the outdoors and spend time in the deer stand, but these days I am more into watching deer than hunting them. My friends are often amazed at the way I deal with the timber rattlesnakes that live on my property. I never kill them, but I do enjoy watching them. When they come into my yard or near my house, I catch them and move them to the back side of my property, where I release them. I collect fine red wines, great sipping whiskeys, and antique firearms. Occasionally, I put on old-fashioned pig pickings, smoking a whole hog and feed more than a hundred guests—Republicans and Democrats, blacks and whites, liberals and conservatives. All I ask is that they leave their political affiliations and egos at the gate when they get here. And we always have a grand time.

I am a high school dropout, a former Klansman and mercenary, an ex-convict and ex-felon. I used to be an extreme racist and ultra-right-wing conservative with no tolerance for those who disagreed with me. I also put myself through college, worked as a hard-nosed environmental regulator, and became the chief operating officer of a company that employed more than a thousand people. I am a nationally recognized authority on environmental emergency response, and I serve as an adviser to many elected officials. All of these things, contradictory though some of them may be, are part of who I've become, and I am proud of that person.

It's Not Over Until It's Over

I took three weeks in September and October 2015 to dedicate some quality time toward the completion of my book. I traveled solo through Wyoming, Montana, and Idaho. I had no set agenda or schedule. I woke up early each morning and started driving with no idea where I would end up that night. Sometimes I found secluded places in the mountains and stopped and began writing.

My accommodations were diverse and often primitive. I spent several days in a nice chateau on Flathead Lake in northwest Montana. Other times I stayed in remote, off-the-grid mountain cabins with no electricity or cellular service or camped under the stars beside my pickup. I spent nights alone in the Wind River Mountains of Wyoming, the Beartooth Mountains of Montana, and the Bitterroot Forest of Idaho with just a sleeping bag, a mattress pad, and a can of grizzly bear repellent. I set up a small folding table and chair as a desk.

I wrote this book because I wanted to show that we are not our pasts. We don't have to be forever linked to our mistakes—or our successes. All of us are going through a process, and none of us has arrived at the end. But most important, I wrote this book to try to give others who may be traveling a very difficult path in life, as I once was, some inspiration and hope. Determination, focus, and hard work can help us overcome some pretty terrible experiences and bad personal traits.

Finally, I wrote this book to try to explain myself—not just to others but to me. It's been quite a ride.

Acknowledgments

I am deeply grateful to Kim Pearson, Mary Miller, and Mary Lauren Boykin, whose help in writing this book made the impossible possible. I also thank Craig Gill, Emily Bandy, and the entire staff at the University Press of Mississippi.

I thank my late parents for putting up with me and for not killing me for all I put them through.

Index